YOUR
MARRIAGE
AND THE
INTERNET

Other books by Thomas Whiteman

Victim of Love? with Randy Petersen
Be Your Own Best Friend with Randy Petersen
Men Who Love Too Little with Randy Petersen
Your Kids and Divorce
Starting Over with Randy Petersen

YOUR
MARRIAGE
AND THE
INTERNET

Thomas Whiteman, Ph.D.
and
Randy Petersen

Fleming H. Revell
A Division of Baker Book House Co
Grand Rapids, Michigan 49516

Published by Fleming H. Revell
a division of Baker Book House Company
P.O. Box 6287, Grand Rapids, MI 49516-6287

Printed in the United States of America

Library of Congress Cataloging-in-Publication Data

Whiteman, Tom
    Your marriage and the internet / Thomas Whiteman and Randy Petersen.
        p.   cm.
    Includes bibliographical references.
    ISBN 0-8007-5765-3
        1. Internet addiction. 2. Marriage counseling. 3. Marriage.
I. Petersen, Randy. II. Title.
RC569.5.I54 W455 2002
616.85′84—dc21   2002004927

For current information about all releases from Baker Book House, visit our web site:
                    http://www.bakerbooks.com

Contents

Acknowledgments

Every book we write is a team effort. This one was especially so. We offer thanks to Deb Stranahan, who got us started with some great web research. Then Kristin Hegar helped by interviewing people and writing up their stories. Kathy deVries provided some case studies and the resource chapter (10). Through it all, Lori Whiteman offered encouragement. As a publisher, Bill Petersen gave us appropriate nudging; as a father, he supplied guidance and support. And Ardythe Petersen helped out with typing and praying. Many thanks to them all. Without them, this book wouldn't exist.

Except where noted, the stories told in this book are true, yet we have changed names and some incidental details to protect the privacy of the people involved. Because of the unique content of this book, we have done much of our research on the Internet. The rapidly changing nature of the web makes it difficult to double-check the stories told there, but those stories parallel the accounts we've heard from our real-life sources. The e-mail or chat room exchanges that begin each chapter are fictitious (except for chapter 7), so don't try to e-mail those fictitious people or visit those fictitious sites. And by the way, use caution in accessing any of the sites mentioned in this book. Some are very good and helpful, but we can't vouch for all the content you'll find. Some good sites are abandoned and taken over by unscrupulous owners. And you never know when a slip of the finger will take you to a web address you don't want to visit. Be wise.

Screened Out
Sarah and John

Sarah was nearing forty when she first brought it up with her husband, John. Their sex life—it wasn't easy to talk about. Married when they were in their young twenties, Sarah and John were both very passionate people. Their relationship was very intense. They enjoyed partying with their friends, and they debated fervently about politics and religion. Their sex life was much like their social life—active, committed, and stimulating.

In her early thirties, Sarah became a Christian. Though John respected her opinion, he did not share her newfound interest in religion. Sarah's incipient spirituality did not create any relationship tension, but it did change her social life. Sarah was not as interested in partying in the old way. It wasn't that she felt these parties were necessarily wrong, but she wanted to express her new beliefs in every aspect of life. That meant some changes in her social lifestyle. John adjusted accordingly. He was getting older and was less interested in the type of parties they had enjoyed when they were first married.

But there was another change that began to happen. Over the following years, their sex life suffered. The frequency of their lovemaking dwindled to once or twice a year.

Comparing notes with some of her friends, Sarah knew that some women lost interest in sex as they aged. Her best friend complained that her husband wanted more sex than she could handle. But it was the opposite situation with Sarah and John. On those rare occasions when they did make love, she was the one to initiate it. She did everything she could to ignite John's desire, but it wasn't there anymore, though he responded politely to her advances. Sarah didn't want politeness; she wanted passion.

Maybe it was a physical problem, she thought. These things happen to men sometimes and they often try to hide it. That could explain John's reluctance. So she finally mentioned her idea to him. He had a physical exam, and the doctor gave him a clean bill of health.

Maybe it was her. Sarah worried that she just wasn't attractive to her husband anymore. But that was especially troubling, because she took good care of herself, working hard to keep her figure. Many men would love to have a woman like her in bed with them, just not the one man she married.

Oh, he was good to her, and he showed affection with occasional kisses and hugs. Sometimes they would snuggle in bed, but that was usually as far as it went. Funny, she thought, her best friend would love to have more snuggling and less sex with her husband. But Sarah was tired of all the foreplay without the *play*. Why wouldn't John deliver?

As the years went on, they developed a pattern that avoided the issue. Sarah went to bed early and arose early. John usually came to bed when she was already asleep and then woke up when she was already downstairs. It was just easier that way. No moments of Will he or won't he? No misread signals. No awkward silences.

But one cold night, Sarah got up to get an extra blanket from the closet in the study. As she opened the door, she saw John in his bathrobe at the computer. On the screen was a picture of a naked woman. John heard her and quickly closed the program, but she had already seen enough. "What's going on, John?" she asked.

He tried to deny it at first, but she wouldn't buy his flimsy explanations. Eventually he admitted that this had become a habit. Two or three times a week he would visit pornographic web sites and masturbate while looking at the pictures. Sarah was horrified and devastated. Clearly this was why he had not been making love with her. He was investing his sexual energy in these computer images, and he had nothing left for her.

Sarah felt angry and frustrated that John had gone to the doctor to check for physical problems, when he knew very well what the problem was. He had let her worry and waste time making appointments, while he was hiding the true cause.

Besides feeling used and deceived, Sarah was disgusted by what John was doing. He was forsaking the marriage bed to fantasize about women who got paid to pose naked. He was pleasuring himself while looking at other people doing things that she was eager to do with him. Why would he do that? What would drive him to that? And how could she hope to compete with those airbrushed pictures of nearly perfect bodies?

Embarrassed and penitent, John promised to stop this habit. He loved her, he said, but he had gotten caught up in this. He really wanted to make their marriage work, but the Internet porn had become so available, so easy. It just sort of happened.

In the following days, John tried hard to make up for his misbehavior, but still the relationship had sunk to a new low. Now John's affectionate touches were repulsive to Sarah. She refused to let him see her naked, not wanting to be compared to pornographic images. But now she felt caught, knowing that her resistance to his touches would make him more inclined to find sexual stimulation on the Internet. So she tried to open up to him, even as he was trying to turn his sexual energy toward her. This was what she had wanted, wasn't it? But now it all felt dirty to her. She hadn't been wildly confident in her femininity before, and now she felt woefully inadequate.

The first time they tried making love, she insisted that they turn out the lights. Even then, as soon as they began intercourse, she began sobbing. Sarah could not stop interpreting John's sexual cues as unwilling or halfhearted. While touching her, was he thinking about other women's bodies? Even in her previous frustration, she had enjoyed their tender times of foreplay, but now she felt that he was just going through the motions. It seemed like a cruel game. Finally, they stopped even trying.

Is there any hope for Sarah and John? We'll return to their story later, but meanwhile we need to talk more about the problem. Their story has been duplicated in thousands of homes. Husbands and wives alike are being caught up in the pornography, sexual chat rooms, and other offerings on the Internet. What is going on?

one

The Lure of the Net

Tigger21: Isn't this great?

Amybelle: What?

Tigger21: E-mail. The whole concept. The technology of instant messages. Here we are conversing as if we're in the same room, but we could be 1000s of miles away.

Amybelle: Or we could be next door neighbors.

Tigger21: Hmmmm. Hadn't thot of that.

In the movie *You've Got Mail,* two people fall in love through e-mail, though in real life they hate each other. The two own rival bookstores. His superstore is putting her mom-and-pop shop out of business. But in the anonymous world of e-mail, Shopgirl and NY152 speak to one another's souls.

"We don't talk about anything personal," the Meg Ryan character explains to a friend. "I don't know his name or where he lives. So it'll be really easy to stop seeing him, because I'm not."

But they *do* talk about personal things—their inner feelings about the events in their lives. "No specifics" is the rule, which is how they avoid finding out each other's true identity, but they connect deeply as they describe themselves in generalities. Shopgirl tells her friend that she wandered into an on-line chat room "for a joke," but then started chatting with this delightful guy. "Books, music, harmless, harmless, meaningless," she says, but we know she's losing her heart to him. After all, it *is* Tom Hanks.

Both characters live with romantic partners, but it's clear that these partners don't really understand them. These relationships function on external commonalities—intelligence or money—but these partners aren't soul mates. We know that Shopgirl and NY152 are meant for each other.

Through all of this, the movie conveys the idea that e-mail somehow cuts through the trivialities of real life and gets to the heart of a relationship. Real-life partners stop paying attention to one another, but, with e-mail, people can share their hearts. In real life, appearance is a major issue. The blind eye of cyberspace gets past that.

Of course, that's not a problem when you're dealing with Meg Ryan and Tom Hanks. Still, the Hanks character shows some trepidation as he's about to see Shopgirl for the first time. "This woman is the most adorable creature I have ever been in contact with," he tells his buddy, "and if she turns out even to be as good-looking as a mailbox, I'd be crazy not to turn my life upside down and *marry* her."

That's the arc that many on-line relationships follow. It's like a pen pal relationship at first. Sight unseen, you develop a mind-to-mind, heart-to-heart relationship. Some are inspired to take it to the next level. Maybe they send pictures of themselves—of course, the best-lit, best-posed photos from ten years ago. Or maybe they just meet.

It is a huge step to move a relationship from cyberspace to real life, and many couples don't survive it. *You've Got Mail* nicely captured the nervousness leading to a first face-to-face meeting. Appearance shouldn't matter so much to us, but it does. We can sense that the Hanks character is giving himself a pep talk, because as jazzed as he is about this soul mate, he really wants her to look beautiful. If Meg Ryan did look like a mailbox, the movie might have ended there.

Seriously, we wonder how the movie would have turned out if she weighed 300 pounds or if he were bald or if their ages were thirty years apart or if she were really a man or if he were a swindler or worse. For every cyber–love story we hear, there are several sadder tales—disappointment, deception, danger. Real life has its shortcomings, but it is better at raising red flags in a relationship. The blind trust of cyber-relationships makes them a risky business.

The Third Wave

It's a revolutionary technology, experts say, just like the printing press. Human communication was transformed with the development of writing, millennia ago, and then again when Johannes Gutenberg invented the printing press in the 1450s. The Internet marks a third wave of human interaction that is washing over the world.

Think about it. Gutenberg wasn't just tinkering around with wood and lead; he was changing civilization. Before he cobbled together that first printing machine, the transfer of ideas went slowly. Scribes could copy manuscripts for the most learned members of society, but generally information passed by word of mouth. Each town was an island, receiving only occasional news from outside. Important ideas—like those of Thomas Aquinas or John Wycliffe—circulated only to university scholars or among church leaders. The information pathway was guarded by gatekeepers, relatively few but quite powerful—those who could read and who could afford those precious handwritten texts.

But Gutenberg's press lit the fuse to an explosion of information. It's no accident that the Protestant Reformation followed shortly thereafter, and then the Renaissance. The act of printing took the power of information away from the leaders of church and society, giving it to anyone who could read the books that were tumbling off the presses.

Gutenberg printed Bibles. Soon Luther was translating the Bible into the common German tongue. Then Protestants across Europe were saying that any believer could understand the Bible without help from a priest. And before long a host of humanists were going outside of Scripture for inspiration. Science, philosophy, history, literature—scholars in every discipline began to explore new ideas, aided by the ease of printing.

The American Revolution got a big boost from cheaply printed pamphlets written by Thomas Paine and others. There was a new democracy at work here. People didn't need those old gatekeepers controlling the flow of information. The new medium of printing opened up a whole new world to the masses.

Let's fast-forward four centuries from Gutenberg into the 1900s. Amazingly the printing press was still the dominant medium. Just before the twentieth century dawned, the United States fought a war that many say was fueled by newspaper headlines: "Remember the Maine!" Later, Communists in Russia won support through (once again) pamphlets; in China it was the printing of a "little red book."

But new media began to take shape in the 1900s. First radio kept Americans up-to-date on the events of World War II. Then television gave us the details of Watergate. In 1991 the TV-watching public actually saw "smart bombs" finding Iraqi targets. Soon we had a whole generation that had learned to read from *Sesame Street*, learned to dance from MTV, and learned to love from *Friends*.

Once again, though, there were gatekeepers. Three big TV networks controlled TV programming for decades, until they were challenged by Fox and cable. Major book publishers controlled the print world. Oh, you could produce your own book, but would anyone buy it? Distribution channels were crowded. Even if you had a book or magazine or radio program or TV show that people wanted, you'd never find your audience unless you got through a gatekeeper—a network, publisher, or distributor.

As it turned out, television was just the kindling for the fiery revolution to come. TV taught us to see life on a screen. The Internet let us interact with that screen.

It's hard to imagine that fifty years ago the computer was just a twinkle in some engineer's eye. Forty years ago a computer would take up a whole room and do less than a single chip can do now. Businesses began to invest in these monster machines, and the engineers kept making them smaller and stronger. It took upstart companies like Apple, Radio Shack, and Commodore to transform this business tool into a household pet. Personal computers flashed on the scene in the 1980s, with the early ones offering a dandy game of Pong.

The Internet began as computer communication among certain universities. Once information was digitized by a computer, it could be translated to sound and sent over phone lines. The government and military jumped in too. It took another upstart company, America Online, to bring the Internet to the general public. Others followed.

The 1990s saw a rapid growth in personal use of the Internet—for business, communication, and entertainment. Suddenly there were no gatekeepers. Well, there were the service providers and the keepers of the domain names, but these generally took a hands-off approach. You could establish a web site with virtually any type of content, and anyone who surfed to your address could see it. E-mail became the new telephone. Search engines could direct you to hundreds, even thousands, of sites on any topic. Chat rooms developed where you could trade information on any topic you wanted, from psychology to sex—especially sex.

By 2000 more than half of U.S. homes had computers (51 percent, up from 42 percent in 1998), and 41.5 percent had Internet access, with that number booming as well (up from 26.2 percent in 1998). These statistics mean that at least 54 million American households have computers and 44 million are on-line.

Just as the printing press changed society, so will the Internet. It is already changing the way people live. E-commerce is the hot new business subject. Any company that has something to sell is seeking to sell it on-line. People are buying books and music, airline tickets and lingerie, groceries and antiques—all by clicking a computer mouse and typing a credit card number. Oh, yes, pornography too.

Early in the Internet revolution, pictures were digitized and sent along with the verbal information. Suddenly pornography had a powerful new outlet. Sexual

It's all too convenient. Many get dragged into Internet porn in just that way. And the push-button life continues within the web. Virtually every site has links to other sites. Click this icon or that one, and you can be led into all sorts of perversions. Relatively tame sites can offer access to wilder sites.

Chat room relationships are a bit less impulsive. You have to invest some time and thought into typing your messages. But the chat room itself is never very far away from you. You might be playing a computer game or paying your bills or checking your e-mail, and you know that a few clicks will open a door into a whole new community, in which you can assume a new identity and carry on intriguing new relationships. Many husbands and wives who never really intended to cheat on their spouse get into these chat rooms innocently, and then are led step-by-step into infidelity. A wife might never think of going on a date with another man or visiting his home, but in a few mouse clicks she can be sharing her secrets with just such a stranger.

The Facade

If computers were advertised as pornography machines, you'd never buy one. If the Internet were dubbed "the superhighway to infidelity," you'd stay away. Of course the technology itself is much more than a smut bearer or marriage breaker. Nowadays you *need* a computer to carry on many tasks in your business and in your life. You have to go on-line to function as a citizen in the twenty-first century. And so every day this basic machine puts you within clicking distance of extremely destructive forces.

Addicts of all sorts form attachments between their "drug of choice" and the delivery systems that supply it.

The alcoholic starts feeling a rush when he passes a bar. The heroin addict might just handle a spoon and sense the familiar craving. I (Tom) have dealt often with the subject of addictive relationships. If you're obsessed with a person, the attachment might be with a certain perfume or type of clothing or the street where you once strolled arm in arm. I regularly counsel relationship addicts to go "cold turkey." They need to stop seeing the person and, as much as possible, avoid the attachment. That is, don't go driving past the person's house. Find a new street to stroll down.

But this becomes difficult when "the street where you live" is the Information Superhighway. If you've grown addicted to a chat room relationship, the best thing is to stop communicating with the person entirely. Stay out of that chat room. Stay out of any chat room. If you're addicted to Internet porn, obviously, stay away from those sites. But the fact is you'll still be throwing yourself into temptation whenever you sit down at the computer to do any legitimate business. Chances are you begin to feel the rush as the computer boots up. You've already attached the computer itself to your addiction. That will make it especially hard to avoid those few easy clicks that get you back into trouble.

How can you go cold turkey when the computer and Internet are such essential parts of modern life? Can you do without them? Maybe. Or maybe you can set some stringent limits on their use.

Practitioners of organized crime learned long ago that they needed a facade as legitimate businesspeople to mask their illegal activities. In a way, the computer world is like that too. The computer is certainly a legitimate tool for business and life, and Internet connections enhance its possibilities. But, especially if you've developed an addiction to its seamier side, you need to be aware how dangerous it is.

New Definitions

Is it cheating if you just talk about sex, if you just type your innermost fantasies on a computer, if you just look at pictures on a web site? These are the moral questions many are asking. The Internet has given us whole new categories of behavior, and the boundaries between good and bad aren't always clear.

While most people would agree that the extremes of sexual interaction on the Internet would constitute infidelity, the questions aren't as easy to answer when taken step by step. Is it wrong for a married person to chat online with a person of the opposite sex? Of course not. But what about when the conversation turns to sex? Or what if it never gets explicit, but the chatters begin to get emotionally involved? At what point does it begin to be cheating?

It's all so new that no one knows the rules. It's easy to rationalize each step until you go too far. "How can it be cheating when I've never actually touched the person?" You can follow that logic all the way through to divorce.

The Promise of Intimacy

Psychologist David Greenfield surveyed eighteen thousand people and found that a major reason people go on-line is to find intimacy.[4] Isn't that ironic? People use an anonymous, faceless communication system to connect with others at the deepest levels. Granted, some are using webcams, with which they can see their correspondent, but for the most part they're just watching words appear on a screen. That's all they know of the person with whom they're trying to find intimacy.

Of course that person could be lying. Face-to-face, we use many lie-detector mechanisms. If a person can't look us in the eye or can't keep a straight face, we know there's a problem. We can sense things from vocal strain or nervous mannerisms. None of these factors is available in an Internet chat, so it's pretty easy for a person to present himself or herself in an entirely false way. That 25-year-old siren that a middle-aged man is about to run away with could easily turn out to be another middle-aged man.

And yet there's something to be said for relationships that aren't based on appearance. Is the faceless Internet chat room really any worse than a soulless singles bar? For people who can't get past hello in a relationship because of their looks or their shyness, the Internet offers an opportunity to connect on a deeper level. From centuries past, we have stories of relationships that were founded on correspondence. The written word allowed people to communicate mind-to-mind, rather than face-to-face. Chat rooms are much the same, only more immediate. And it's true that some solid relationships have been forged there.

Such relationships might be deeper than those found at singles bars, and the participants often exult in that depth. "I can really be myself, without worrying about how I look." The chat room seems to take things to a new level, where people really listen to what you're saying, rather than judging you on shallow criteria. And that may be true. But the "intimacy" of the Internet chat room is still a partial thing. You don't know for sure that the person on the other side of cyberspace is being honest with you. The chat room still allows a person to put his best phrase forward.

The Promise of Escape

Marriage is hard work. We've talked with thousands of couples who have struggled to maintain their vows, and thousands of others who have succumbed to divorce. The union of two different people is a wonderful thing, but it has its difficulties too. We probably don't need to tell you that.

One reason many marriages stay together is that they're hard to get out of. We don't mean to be too cynical here, but it's true. Husbands and wives knit their lives together, and divorce requires an unraveling. Children, house, belongings, patterns of life, and so on—the divvying up of all of this is usually harder than staying married. But what if someone showed up with a plane ticket to a new life somewhere else? All expenses paid. Leave behind the struggles of your marriage. It would be very tempting, wouldn't it? The Internet is that plane ticket.

Want sexual images that your spouse can't provide? The net is crammed with them. Want someone to listen to the longings of your heart? Pick a chat room and start typing. The net offers escape from the mundane stuff of life. That Microsoft slogan of a few years back was well-chosen—"Where do you want to go today?" You can stamp this ticket for virtually anywhere.

"My husband and I were happily married for twelve years, or so I thought," wrote one troubled wife, "until we got the computer a year ago. It started out as fun, surfing the net, exploring the world, and then we found the chat rooms. At first it was fun, talking to people all over the country and the world. But then I started noticing that he was on the computer *all* the time, every spare minute. Talking in chat rooms to women. When I would walk in the room or near the computer, he would get irritated, minimize the screen, act real nervous."

One day this husband went to work and didn't come home. Police found his car at the airport. The wife began contacting on-line chat partners, asking for clues, and one of them responded that he had mentioned running off with another woman he had met in a chat room. Shortly after that, he called home. Yes, that's exactly what had happened. His Internet adventure had turned into a real-life escape. Amazingly he decided to come home and seek counseling with his wife to try to restore their marriage. "He does not go on the computer any more at all," his wife notes.[5]

In real life, extramarital affairs are seldom about sex. That might surprise you, but it's true. In counseling, we're more apt to hear statements like, "My lover listens to me, and my husband stopped doing that a while ago." Or, "This other woman accepts me for who I am." People have affairs with people who meet the needs their spouse isn't meeting. That's what makes Internet chat rooms so innocently dangerous. It's just people talking. But the fact is that many married people go on-line to find the intimacy they don't find in their marriage. They're seeking to meet some need that's not getting met by their spouse. Rather than working through their marital frustrations, they are escaping to the Shangri-la of cyberspace, where they can be anybody and meet anybody.

Models of Addiction

Experts have been analyzing Internet addiction in recent years. Obviously this is a new syndrome, but it fits into many traditional models of addiction. Dr. Kimberly Young, founder and president of the Center for On-Line Addiction, talks about the ACE model, which "examines the *Anonymity* of on-line interactions that serves to increase the likelihood of the behavior, the *Convenience* of cyberporn and sexually oriented chat rooms making it easily available to users, and finally the *Escape* from mental tension derived from the experience which serves to reinforce the behavior leading to compulsivity."[6]

Dr. Mark Laaser, an expert in the area of sexual addiction, has a similar model: The Internet is accessible, affordable, and anonymous. "We are experiencing an epidemic of people becoming addicted to sex on their personal and business computers," he writes.[7]

Imagine a drug advertised to change you into anyone you wanted to be. In your new persona, the ads would declare, you could have amazing experiences with exciting people. You could enjoy a whole new life. And you could have as much of this drug as you could consume, at essentially no cost. Pushers will deliver this drug to your door discreetly, twenty-four hours a day, and no one needs to know that you're taking it. This drug would be highly addictive, wouldn't it?

And that's pretty much what the Internet offers, through chat rooms and other sex sites. As with any drug, the benefits are hyped and the costs are ignored. You might pay for this "drug" with broken relationships. It might wreck your marriage. It might make you less satisfied with your real self. It might demand more and more of your time and energy and thought life. It'll change you, all right, but you won't like the results. Addiction rewires your brain. It changes your priorities. Everything that's good in your life will be seen through the lens of your Internet addiction—as if you're on the inside of that screen looking out.

In this book we're not just talking about sexual addiction, though it is a major component of the problem. We're concerned with any way in which the Internet can affect your marriage. It may be the explicit, obscene lure of cyberporn, or it may be the tamer attraction of heart-to-heart chats. It may just be the preoccupation with fantasy football or stock quotes or eBay. If it takes you away from your marriage, it's a problem.

Chances are you've got a ferocious tiger in your home. It could eat you alive, so you'd better make sure it's on a strong leash.

two[

Not
All Bad

Subj: Hi
Date: 5/12/02 2:58:47 PM Eastern Daylight Time
From: Jomogo@aol.com
To: PDaddy99@earthlink.net

Just saying hi, Dad. Got back from my week at the shore with Kate
and the kids. Had a great time. I'll e-mail you some of the pictures.
Don't worry: they'll be smaller this time. They won't take a day and
a half to download.

How was your time with Aunt Helen? We were praying for you. And
for her.

I was just thinking. Thank God for e-mail. We used to talk—
what?—twice a year? I'm so bad about calling, I know. But this

makes it easy. It's good to be in touch with you more. My love to Mom.

When the telephone was invented, some people were sure it would ruin everything. Radio was branded as "a tool of the devil." Motion pictures, some warned, would unleash the worst passions of humanity. Television would mean the end of civilization as we know it. Were they right?

Well . . . no. Every new technology is met with some resistance. People attach all sorts of moral issues to the newest gadgets, when the truth is that they're just gadgets. Technology doesn't corrupt people; *people* corrupt people. Technology just makes it easier.

So as our lives begin to adapt to the Internet (just as human life has previously adapted to the telephone and TV), we want to avoid the errors of those who hate technological advances precisely because they are technological advances. We can embrace the ways the Internet makes our lives better, even as we remain alert to its dangers.

Thanks to the Internet, these words you're reading are being typed only once. We authors will send this document over the Internet to each other and to the publisher, who will have it edited on a computer and typeset for printing—all without much retyping. It wasn't always that way.

Just fifteen years ago, as Randy began his freelance writing career, he typed articles on an electric typewriter and sent the pages through the mail. Those pages were edited by hand and retyped for printing. On deadline, he'd rush out to the FedEx office for overnight delivery of those pages. Now, those "pages" are just computer files, not pieces of paper, and they're delivered instantly on-line.

So obviously we're grateful for the way the Internet has made our work more efficient. In addition, much of the research for this book has been done over the Internet. Rather than burrowing away in libraries for a few afternoons, we can sit at our computers night or day and get access to the latest information. Once again, the web helps us.

We have also benefited from the convenience of e-mail. Tom has a nine-to-five job running several counseling offices. He also has a family, and he tries to preserve his time with them as much as possible. Randy is single and works at home, so he's writing at all hours of the day or night. In other words, our schedules don't exactly coincide. Yet we stay in touch through answering machines and e-mail.

You have probably experienced the same thing in your work and relationships. The Internet has made our lives easier in many ways, and in some cases it has made our lives better. So we're not saying the whole technology is evil. We're not trying to shut down this superhighway— as if we could.

Opening Options

The Internet is here to stay, at least until it gets co-opted by a newer technology, which will also have dangers. We need to learn to live with it, steering clear of the pitfalls while using it to improve our lives—perhaps even using it to improve our marriages.

We have found that it's best to take a positive approach to a problem. If you focus on the bad things, you become obsessed with them and you never find a way around them. It's better to take note of the dangers but then seek positive alternatives.

There's a sad irony about any addiction. People think they're being free, when they are actually becoming enslaved. Drugs, drink, gambling, you name it—addicts wave their free will like a flag. If a loved one tries to intervene, the addict cries foul. "You're trying to restrict my freedom!" But it's actually the addiction that's restricting the addict's freedom. The only choice is *more*.

We see this especially with sex addiction in its various forms—pornography, infidelity, prostitution, and so on. The more you indulge, the less it means. A person may be trying to throw off restraints and enjoy sex freely, but he or she is actually becoming a slave, with more restraints. And the beautiful gift of sex, intended to be enjoyed within the committed relationship of marriage, is lost.

The Internet promises freedom. If you've seen any tech commercials over the last five years or so, you know the key word is *free*—not free of cost, but free of restraint, free to explore, free to break boundaries. All sorts of songs from the liberty-loving sixties have been trotted out to celebrate our new frontier. It's the freedom to be anyone, see anything, go anywhere, know anything. That's the promise.

As we indicated in the last chapter, those far-reaching claims make the Internet especially addictive. And, as with any other addiction, the promise of freedom melts into the reality of bondage. The Internet addict ignores a million sites that can educate, edify, and entertain and chooses only the sites that indulge his or her shallow lusts. The problem with Internet addicts is not that they're too free, but that they're not free enough. The Internet offers us an exciting new frontier, almost as exciting as real life. Can we exercise the freedom to explore all the good things we can find there?

You can preach to an alcoholic every day about the evils of drinking, but eventually all that preaching starts to backfire. The person begins to obsess about the thing he's not allowed to have. Obsession becomes temptation. One's whole life is now about alcohol—drinking it or not drinking it. The most successful recovery involves opening up the rest of life, giving a person other activities and interests so that he or she can forget about the addiction for a while.

That's basically what our Internet strategy should be. Increasingly, human life will be lived in, on, and around the Internet (or its successors). While there are destructive elements on the web we should avoid, there are also valuable elements. So, while we do recommend cold-turkey detachment for the most compulsive net users, we also celebrate the responsible use of Internet resources—in balance with real-life experiences—to help us grow in our personal lives and relationships.

What's good about the Internet? How can it help us improve our lives? We've boiled it down to three broad categories: information, commerce, and connection.

Information

The Internet is the biggest, fastest-growing library the world has ever seen. You could spend a lifetime sifting through the information it contains and still barely make a dent in it. And it's just getting started. In the coming years there will be even more resources available on-line—every book published, every magazine, every doctoral thesis, the latest scientific data. The Internet is already making many previous information channels obsolete. Book publishers wonder how long it will be before the paper-and-ink versions of their products go the way of the dinosaur. Public libraries are fast becoming Internet centers.

So if your kid wants help with homework, it's there, somewhere. You still have to find it. Search engines like Yahoo or Alta Vista help you find what you want, but they're likely to give you three hundred sources when you need only three. You can find every site that mentions a key word or phrase or name, but how can you find the sites that will be truly helpful? And how can you decide which information is truly reliable? How do you know you're not getting propaganda or half-baked theories?

Basically what we have here is a giant, well-catalogued pile of information. What the Internet lacks is wisdom. We see this with the recent difficulties in screening Internet use in public libraries. Most people want to shield children from obscene materials, and so legislation has been put forward to require public libraries to install programs on their computers that block obscene content. Sounds good, but opponents point out that such programs also screen out some beneficial sites, such as those providing information on breast cancer. It's a tough question, as it turns out. A computer program can distinguish between "good" words and "bad" words, but it can't decide what's truly good for you.

The next few years, we believe, will see the emergence of various gatekeepers on the Internet. Search engines might be set up by some university or think tank that will screen out the nonsense and propaganda sites. You'll get smaller piles of information, but you'll find it more reliable. Already we're seeing some Christian service providers and child-friendly programs for home computers that block access to obscene material. They may not be perfect, but many families are willing to give up access to certain information to keep harmful material out of their homes.

The Internet offers a vast array of knowledge. Web users should be the smartest people on earth. People who use it to focus on smut or mindless chats could be benefiting from the web—finding out how the weather works, learning how to fix their car, studying the history of their town or the genealogy of their family. Those who use the Internet can enroll in an on-line college course or even learn more about their faith.

The Pew Center for Research sponsored a study that found 20 percent of U.S. net users getting religious or spiritual information on-line. That makes those subjects more popular than on-line banking (18 percent) or on-line auctions (15 percent). In the last three months of the year 2000, about twenty million people sought spiritual information over the Internet. In addition, the Internet has become a valuable church resource, with 81 percent of clergy using it to gain information for worship services.[1]

There is also information about marriage and family life. Of course, many books have been published over the years about strengthening marriages. We've written a few ourselves. Increasingly that information is going on-line. You can learn from leading psychologists how to avoid relational pitfalls and how to cement your commitment.

Whatever information you gather on the web, share it with your spouse and family. If one of the dangerous aspects of the Internet is its privacy, you can combat that by being very open about what you're learning there.

Commerce

Internet commerce has posed some interesting questions over the last decade. Will people buy something they can't take off a shelf and hold in their hands? Will the Internet ever be secure enough to manage risk-free credit card transactions? Is there enough of a market to justify the start-up costs of an Internet site? Will Internet business threaten real-life stores?

The answers have been coming back: yes, yes, yes, and yes. The Internet is revolutionizing business. Shopping at home is easy and comfortable, once you get past your reluctance to give out a credit card number. Selection is broad, and you can compare costs to get the best deal. And auction services like eBay can make the process fun too. Retailers who use the Internet can avoid warehousing costs, not to mention the upkeep of store maintenance and personnel. The web can match the right consumer with the right product anywhere in the world. Then it's just a matter of cost and shipping.

Of course there are glitches. The Romans used to say, *Caveat emptor*—let the buyer beware. If that was true in the old Forum, it's even more important in this new forum of business. You can't see the person on the other end of the transaction. How do you know you won't get rooked? Established companies have a name and a history to back them up, but smaller new Internet companies don't, and person-to-person exchanges are always iffy. Horror stories abound.

But the problems with the new commerce haven't overshadowed its success. This is clearly the wave of the future. We'll be buying more and more on-line.

Connection

At this point, however, the greatest impact of the Internet has occurred in interpersonal communication. E-mail, instant messages, chat rooms, newsgroups, matchmaking services—this is the nerve system of a new body of computer users.

Ten-year-olds rush home from school to check their e-mail and to chat on-line with the friends they just saw at school.

Teenagers do research on the Internet, but also check to see what "buddies" are on-line. They share instant messages back and forth. The content is seldom earth shattering. IMs are usually just "Hi, how ya doin'?" and mundane news of the day. But it's like having a friend sitting with you at a library table, only there's no librarian to shush you.

Busy singles tap into matchmaking sites, getting e-addresses of people who share their interests, and beginning e-mail correspondences.

Churches are waking up to the value of e-mail. The Pew Center survey finds that 82 percent of clergy use e-mail to connect with parishioners, and nearly half of them e-mail other clergy.[2] The bulky logistics of mass mailings to the church list are being replaced by an easier, cheaper alternative: the e-mailing. At Randy's church, an administrator became aware of a major financial need by a church member that had to be met immediately. She put out the word via e-mail. The next day there were three checks on her desk; within the week, thousands of dollars were raised. Without the immediacy of e-mail, that need would not have been met as quickly as required.

We're also seeing more and more churches with web sites. This just takes connection to a new level. Members can dial up and read the list of church activities or prayer requests. Visitors can learn the times of services and get directions. Pastors' messages can be available in print, audio, or streaming video (or perhaps screaming video, if that's the pastor's style).

We, Tom and Randy, have found that e-mail helps us keep in touch with extended family and distant friends. Of course, we *could* call, and we do sometimes, but that's a commitment of time and energy that we can't always make. E-mail is great for the short message, the "just thinking of you" note, the news item, the dumb joke. You can send it anytime, and the message is read at a convenient time for the receiver.

In New Jersey a court ruled that a divorced woman could move across the country with her daughter, even though she shared custody with the father, who remained in New Jersey. The judge said the father could keep in touch through e-mail. We're not supporting the wisdom of that decision, but it does indicate a modern trend. E-mail is considered virtually equivalent to face-to-face communication.

Speaking of modern trends, here's another: The Internet has shrunk the world. Just three generations ago, communication from one continent to another took months, as a ship carried a letter across the ocean. The telegraph and then the wireless began to change that. One generation ago, you could make a call across the ocean, but it would be very expensive and the connection might not be so great. Now you can send a message across the world as easily as you can send it across the street. That "send" button beneath your cursor connects you with anyone on earth who has a modem.

That means you can keep in touch with friends who have moved abroad, with missionaries your church supports, or with computer "pen pals" from other lands. You can expand your horizons in more ways than one.

Ken and Maureen found each other through an on-line dating service early in the year 2000. On the last day of that year, they got married. Maureen moved from Johannesburg, South Africa, to Ken's home in rural New Hampshire. "We were 150 percent honest with each other," Maureen said of their computer courtship. "We are also perfectly at ease with being by ourselves. . . . Most important of all—to me—is that we share the same spiritual views."[3]

The Ken and Maureen story is notable because of its distance and its speed. In previous generations, if they had met at all, their courtship would have involved letters written back and forth and perhaps a few expensive trips across the globe. The Internet allowed them to condense all of that into less than a year. And note Maureen's emphasis on inner issues—honesty, independence, spirituality. She's not saying, "Ken's so cute," because the relationship was built before they had seen each other. This is not following the dangerous myth of "love at first sight." If anything, it's love at first byte. That, of course, has different dangers.

"I was living in York, Pennsylvania, when I met my on-line love," writes Nicole. "He IM'd me after reading my profile. We became very close and decided (before we ever met) that we wanted to live together. . . . I set off driving by myself to meet him in Topeka, Kansas." She goes on to tell a sweet story about how she got as far as Missouri and was too tired to go on. He drove three hundred miles through bad weather and worse traffic to meet her there. "I went straight into his arms and cried. We've been together ever since."[4]

Apparently geography is no object when you find true love in cyberspace. It all sounds great, until you realize that Nicole was already married—to someone else. Apparently her wedding vows were no object either. "I was married at sixteen and the relationship was falling apart before my eyes," she added. "I was searching for someone, for something. I found it in Dave. For the first time in months I smiled, laughed, wanted to share my life with someone again."

We just found this story on a web site, and we don't know all that was going on in Nicole's life, so we're hesitant to comment on the specifics of her story. But we know this happens with many marital breakups. A spouse is unhappy; a relationship is falling apart. Who knows whether the marriage could be restored if they worked at it? Sadly, they never get the chance. One spouse strikes up a cyber-romance with someone who seems to be an ideal mate—everything the current partner is not. Next thing you know, you're headed for Kansas.

That's the thing about connections. They can be good or bad. For every Ken and Maureen, there's a Nicole and Dave. We also wonder, with both couples, how long the honeymoon will last. Will they still be "150 percent honest with each other" when they're sharing three meals a day? Will Nicole ever go looking for a new cyberpartner who's everything that Dave fails to be?

Still, we're encouraged that Maureen and Ken highlight the importance of shared spiritual views. In the modern dating scene, it's hard for single people to find others with whom they're spiritually compatible. Singles bars aren't the most soul-inspiring places. If you can use a computer to weed out the time-wasters, why not? If an on-line dating service can connect you with a kindred spirit who shares your faith and values, then go for it.

But not if you're already married.

Denise was at the end of her rope. This stay-at-home mom browsed to an America Online site for people like her, and she posted a long, rambling message about her frustrations. A woman named Viv answered her with a message of encouragement. As they e-mailed back and forth, they found that their lives were amazingly similar. Both were married, with two kids the same ages, who were athletic, creative, and terrible at spelling. They quickly developed a strong friendship.

Viv writes that the level of honesty in this e-mail correspondence is like nothing she has experienced in real life. Thoughts, spirituality, moods, which take time to explore and organize, don't fit well into phone chats or lunch dates. Viv says, "When I am typing a letter to Denise, I can FINISH a thought. Interruptions may happen, but I can just go back to where I was and continue." She also notes that she feels freer to talk about spiritual issues on-line.[5]

So, of course, on-line interpersonal connections aren't always romantic. Good friendships can be forged as well.

A Christian web site includes a story of a young woman, a college student, who met a guy in an interactive area of a web site for a Christian rock group. "They traded messages about the band's lyrics and eventually delved into theological issues," reported a concerned friend. Over the next month, the friendship deepened. It was completely platonic, based on spiritual issues, but it also took a lot of time. "It began to cut into her friendships," the friend notes. "Although she was talking about God a lot—she was too distracted by her e-mail to spend time with Him." The young woman eventually had to end the correspondence and get on with her life.[6]

We wouldn't be quite so hard on this young woman. College students are *supposed* to spend hours sitting around talking about spirituality and theology. That's what they do. If it's on a computer, so what? And yet we understand that computer chats can be habit-forming— even if you're chatting about good things. Everyone needs to keep life in balance.

Fire!

The Internet is an extremely powerful force in modern life—like fire. Is fire a good thing or a bad thing? That depends on whom you ask. Talk to the family who just saw their house go up in flames after an electrical short, and they'll tell you how bad fire is. But talk to the guy trying to light charcoal for a backyard barbecue, and he's all for it.

Fire is a powerful force that can be used for good or bad. So is the Internet. With its fountain of information, its burgeoning commerce, and its widespread connections, the Internet is here to stay. It will be part of our lives and increasingly so. But how will we use it? Will we let it burn down our marriages, our families, our balanced lives? Or will we use it to nourish our souls, to make new friends, to grow into better people?

Those are the questions we must answer.

Fragmenting a Family
Tony and Evelyn

Tony says he and Evelyn were the "ideal couple" for twenty years. Then they got a computer. At first it was fun to look up various subjects on the Internet. Their two kids were teenagers, with various school papers to do, and they could do their research on-line. Tony and Evelyn even experimented with chat rooms for a while. They would talk about the interesting folks they met there. It was all in good fun.

The novelty wore off for Tony. He'd use the computer for basic e-mail, and that was about it. Besides, it seemed Evelyn was on it all the time. Though she had a full-time job, she still managed to put in another fifty hours a week at the computer, traveling the Information Superhighway.

That meant fifty hours she was not spending with Tony, and he resented it. They began to argue more frequently, though they had enjoyed a rather peaceful marriage up to that point. She accused him of having an affair. He suspected that *she* was the philandering one. They had always shared hello-and-goodbye kisses, but now she would turn her head. When he asked about this, Evelyn confessed that she was "falling out of love" with him.

Something was going on, and Tony figured it had to do with the Internet. That was when he learned how to check the memory files on the computer, which store records of Internet activity. He was able to track the chat rooms Evelyn visited. It seems that she had flirted with a number of men in different chat rooms, but then she zeroed in on one particular boyfriend. When she suddenly left for a "training seminar" in another state, Tony knew she was going to meet him. Later he intercepted some e-mail greetings from the man, including phrases such as "hugs, kisses, and fondles" and "I can't wait for you to rub your hands on my body." This was no platonic pen pal.

The whole family noticed the change in Evelyn as she became more and more addicted. Though they kept the computer in the kitchen at first, their machine soon became *her* machine. She added a camera and headphones and would stay at the computer most nights until three or four in the morning. One night their son woke up and went to the kitchen for something to drink. He saw his mother in her bathrobe in front of the computer. The green eye of the camera mounted on the computer was on. The screen showed a man wearing only boxer shorts. She had her headset on and was conversing with him. Transfixed, the boy overheard his mother describe the sexual activity she was imagining with this man. When her son confronted Evelyn about it the next day, she insisted he hadn't seen anything. Soon after that, she moved the computer to another room.

Evelyn's relationship with Tony kept deteriorating. He wanted to see a marriage counselor, but she didn't. Though she went with him to one session, she refused to return. Eventually she moved to a different bedroom, taking the computer with her. Now, though living in the same house for economic reasons, they were legally separated. Tony would hear the sounds of cybersex coming from her room at all hours of the night.

A year and a half after the separation began, Evelyn's on-line boyfriend had a heart attack and died. She grieved as if she'd been married to him. But if Tony harbored any hopes that he and Evelyn would get back together, these were quickly dashed. She turned to her chat room partners for support. In fact some even sent her sympathy cards. "That was weird," says Tony, "living in the same house and seeing sympathy cards coming in the mail for your wife because her boyfriend died." Within six more months, they were divorced.

"I wish we had set a time limit on computer use when we first got it," Tony says now. "She was on the computer in the morning and then would come home during lunch break to get on-line and then the second she got home from work she'd be back on the computer again. The Internet was her number one top priority."

Maybe the marriage was doomed anyway. Maybe she would have had an affair with someone else or fallen prey to some other addiction.

Who knows? But Tony can't help but think that the computer was the culprit. The Internet led his wife away from him.

He also worries about the lasting effect on their children. Evelyn has custody of their daughter, now eighteen. Tony keeps in touch, mostly through e-mail. He senses that Evelyn has been bad-mouthing him and suspects that their daughter has been following in her mother's footsteps, visiting chat rooms for sexually explicit conversations.

Their son, now in college, talks with his mother occasionally and says there are no hard feelings, but he admits he has huge trust issues as he enters any new relationship with a woman. And he hates computers. He'll use the ones in the school library only when necessary and he checks his e-mail rarely. "My only regret in this whole situation," he says, "is that I didn't take a shotgun and shoot the computer."

three[

His
Needs,
Her
Needs

lizbet: You guys. You think the Internet is your personal playground.

inkster5: what's that supposed to mean?

lizbet: You're always bragging about your bigger modems and your faster speeds.

polyesterC: Boys and their toys

inkster5: well if it weren't for men there wouldn't be an internet

brandonn: Or the info superhighway would go really slow.

lizbet: No, I think it would be faster without men.

brandonn: Everyone driving with their turn signals on ;)

inkster5: faster? how?

lizbet: We wouldn't have all those porn sites clogging up the wires.

A few years ago, we were writing a book about the emotional and relational differences between men and women. It was a fascinating time of research, and both of us found ourselves explaining our theories to friends and associates. Randy, for instance, mentioned to his friend Kim that men and women tend to carry on conversations with different body language. Go to a party and you'll see men standing side by side, or at least angled outward, scoping out the room, while women tend to talk face-to-face, squared away in focused conversations.

Not long after that, Kim came back and told Randy, "When you were saying that, I thought it was just another half-baked theory of yours. But then I went to a party and I saw exactly what you said. Nine times out of ten, men were side by side and women face-to-face. It was amazing."

Sure, we have our share of half-baked theories, but this one is well-founded: Men and women tend to operate differently. We understand the political history involved here. For centuries, no one would have squawked about the idea of men and women being different. But the feminist revolution of the 1970s taught us to beware of prejudice. Often men in power have used gender differences to keep women out of power. It was suddenly very important to show that women were equal to men in every way.

But equal doesn't mean identical. By the 1990s there were a lot of confused couples who were trying to relate on an equal basis but denying the basic differences that allowed them to complement one another. Everyone sort of knew the differences, but it wasn't proper to talk about them.

Finally some psychologist-authors broke the silence, among them Willard Harley with *His Needs, Her Needs;* John Gray with *Men Are from Mars, Women Are from Venus;* and Deborah Tannen with *You Just Don't Understand.* Nowadays some are still leery of the emphasis on gender differences, but at least people are talking about them.

So as we plunge into a discussion of the different ways men and women interact on the Internet, we need to make a few things clear. First, by saying the sexes tend to be different, we're not establishing one as better than the other. We're not implying that the general way that women use the Internet is any better than the way men use it or vice versa.

Second, we're talking about *tendencies*. This doesn't mean that every man does one thing and every woman does another (or that there's something wrong with you if you don't fit the pattern). There are always exceptions. We're just hoping that these generalities may help you understand your specific situation.

Third, there is a growing body of research on this matter. Brain studies, for instance, have found that women have more connective fibers between the hemispheres. Since one half of the brain governs speech and the other is the emotional center, that may suggest that women are naturally better at communicating their emotions. Maybe. The research is still pretty new, but there are some intriguing theories that give scientific reasons for tendencies we've already observed.

Fourth, there's always a scientific debate between nature and nurture. Are we born this way, or do we learn certain behaviors? We generally accept both explanations—nature *and* nurture—but that question is really not important for our purposes. We are interested in the way things are, not how they got that way.

Women's Intuition

So why do men stand side by side at parties while women stand face-to-face? Because men are scanners while women are readers. Men sweep across a scene, getting the lay of the land, assessing the big picture. Women connect with individual people, listening to their words, reading their body language.

After such a party, a couple might discuss the information they gathered.

She: So how's Bill?

He: All right, I guess.

She: You guess? You were talking with him for an hour.

He: He seemed fine.

She: What did you talk about?

He: Nothing much.

She: For an hour?

He: We talked about sports a little and business.

She: Did he say anything about his marriage being in trouble?

He: No. Is his marriage in trouble?

She: I don't know but—

He: You were talking with Jan. What did she say?

She: Nothing specifically, but I could tell she was worried.

He: You could tell? How?

She: I could just tell. Women's intuition.

He: Oh, that. What exactly did Jan say?

She: Nothing, really.

He: Nothing?

She: I asked her how things were with Bill, and she said they were fine.

He: So of course you knew there was something wrong.

She: Exactly.

He: She said they were fine!

She: Exactly. Not "great." Not "wonderful." Just "fine." There's got to be something wrong.

He: That's crazy.

She: Besides, it was the *way* she said it. She let me know they were in trouble.

He: Oh, so she wanted you to know.

She: Right.

He: So she said they were fine.

She: Exactly. I mean, she couldn't really come out and *tell* me.

He: Of course not.

She: Not at a party. But we'll have lunch next week. Then she'll tell me.

He: Maybe she'll tap it out in Morse code with her spoon.

She: Very funny. I can't believe Bill didn't say anything to you. In a whole hour you didn't even ask about his family?

He: Come to think of it, I did ask him about Jan and the kids.

She: And?

He: He said they were fine.

She: See?

If you're a man reading that, you understand the frustration of the man in the scene. Women are always reading between the lines, sensing things that aren't openly stated. They appeal to women's intuition, as if it's a code that unlocks the secrets of the universe. If you're a man in relationship with an especially perceptive woman, her mind reading abilities can be scary. It might gall you that she presumes to know what you're thinking, but it's even worse when she's right.

If you're a woman reading the scene, you probably recognize that old male insensitivity. How can two men be friends with each other and never talk about anything important? How can men be smart in so many areas of life but ignorant about people? Why don't they see what you see?

Men and women tend to gather and process information in different ways. Men seek out the *facts* of a situation, while women get a *feel* for it. In conversation men usually hear what's said, while women perceive the whole presentation. Usually understanding the truth of a matter requires some of both approaches. Sometimes women read things into a situation—their intuition steers them wrong. But sometimes men miss the whole message, because they're hearing only the words.

Other Differences

There are many other ways in which the genders tend to differ in thought and personality. It may be helpful to consider some of these as we look at the different ways men and women use the Internet.

Men compartmentalize. Women mix everything together. Men's brains are offices with cubicles. Women's are living rooms. If it's true that women have more connecting fibers in the brain, that might explain it. Everything *is* mixed together for them, while men's thoughts inhabit a collection of islands.

This quality helps men turn off their emotions to complete a task. It also might make men better at having (and hiding) affairs. They think they can conduct a normal marriage in one compartment of the brain, while they fool around in another cubicle. Women might try this, but they have a harder time keeping things separate.

Infidelity is just one example of *moral* compartmentalization. Often men have secret corners of their lives they just sort of wall off from the rest. They may be upstanding citizens, but in certain times and places they can become quite different.

Women tend to be more verbal than men. Sure, there are talkative men and shy women, but on the whole, women have more connection between their feelings and their language. Randy was about two years old before he started talking, causing concern for his parents. But one day he just uttered a complete sentence, as if he didn't want to speak at all unless he had something good to say. Many men are like that. They develop their sentences first and then deliver them. Women are more apt to put an idea out there and *then* develop it.

Women are more relational than men. Of course women bear children and nurse them, giving them a head start in the nurturing department. Mothers develop a symbiotic bond with their children that starts in the womb and continues afterward. When a baby is goo-gooing incomprehensibly, the mother is more likely to understand what he or she needs. Mothers learn to read their children in ways that fathers can't.

It seems that this people-reading ability gets transferred to the wider world. Women tend to be better than men at developing emotional bonds with others. Women are more apt to define themselves in terms of relationship. Ask a man to introduce himself, and he'll probably start with his job; ask a woman, and she'll probably start with her family.

Men tend to be more aggressive, competitive, and goal-oriented. Blame this on testosterone, the male hormone. Men like to win. Men are more likely to develop that tunnel vision that focuses on the prize, ignoring everything else along the way. This doesn't mean that women can't compete with men—say, in business—but women are more likely to view success in noncompetitive ways. They're more apt to seek relational solutions that meet broader goals.

Men like control and independence. Once again we must state that there are many exceptions, but we do observe a tendency in men to go it alone. We think it's a combination of their competitive instincts and their comparative lack of relational skill. If women are better at some game, men don't want to play it. That's a simplification, to be sure, but we often see this in the communication game or the relationship game. Since women are naturally and culturally prepared to excel in these areas, men withdraw.

The Sexes and the Internet

What happens, then, when men and women log on the Internet?

The computer is essentially a guy's kind of machine. It has no intuition. It deals in basic facts. Whatever you type in, that's what the computer "hears." If you misspell a web address, the computer won't "know" what you meant. It takes what you give it at face value. (Advances in artificial intelligence may be changing that, but for now the computer's perception is pretty basic.)

So it's no surprise that, in their early years, personal computers were used by men in overwhelming proportions. Women couldn't be bothered with them. Let the man play with his new toy; the woman had more important things to do.

But with the advent of the Internet, the computer suddenly became a very different kind of machine. Now it could be a tool for relationships, as well as a source of information. E-mail could keep people in touch and chat rooms could create new friendships. The Internet became women's territory as much as it was men's. And the statistics showed it. Women's use of computers has risen rapidly in the last few years, recently surpassing that of men.

So let's talk about how men and women use the web differently.

Chat Rooms

If you're into relationships, a chat room is good news and bad news. The good news is that you can converse with a broad range of people on just about any subject. The bad news is that you're never sure whom you're talking with. A chat room gives amazing access to people from different cultures, with different experiences, having different ideas, but you can't read their body language. You never know exactly where they're coming from.

And that neutralizes some of the advantage that women usually have in conversation. As we saw in the "he/she" dialogue earlier in the chapter, the man was focusing on what was literally said, while the woman gathered a lot from *how* something was said. Computer conversation fits more into the man's style. What you see is what you get—words on a screen.

That also plays into a man's need for control. Some who get tongue-tied in personal conversations can find release in the ability to backspace over a computer comment. Remember that men like to process their words before they utter them. The structure of computer chatting helps them do that.

So chat rooms attract women with the promise of human relationships, but their dynamics seem to level the playing field, giving men more of an ability to express themselves in ways with which they're comfortable. And that may be why some women get drawn away from their real relationships in favor of their connections with men on the Internet. It's not just "the lure of the other." They may actually find a deeper level of communication on the computer. Why? Because the chat rooms offer men a comfort zone that face-to-face relationships don't have.

Brett was a pretty typical guy. He could talk for hours about sports or business but not about his feelings. His wife, Carol, knew he loved her but she wished he would say it more often. She remembered their courtship, how open he seemed to be. Back then they would spend many relaxed hours together, learning about each other. He would talk about his feelings for her, and all his feelings, but something changed after they got married. He closed up.

In private counseling, Brett began to slowly express some of his feelings. He had buried them so deep, it took a while to dig them up. And when he did, his emotions confused him. He loved Carol deeply, but he also felt some resentment over his lost freedom. He couldn't really talk to her about that; it would hurt her. He also had some insecurities about his job, but whenever he tried to talk about those feelings, Carol would jump furiously into the conversation, finishing his sentences, evaluating what he said—almost before he said it. She was like a parched desert traveler, lapping up any trickle of water. He learned to keep those feelings to himself.

Whenever he mused about doing something—starting a project around the house, volunteering in the community, or even looking for a new job—she would begin planning it. Suddenly it became her dream not his. Then she would ask him about it the following week and the next week and the next week. She meant well, but he felt nagged. He needed time to develop those thoughts on his own.

As Carol met with the counselor, she expressed her frustration. Brett was a locked safe, and she had forgotten the combination. She wanted the kind of free-flowing conversation they had enjoyed before their marriage. She didn't want to live like this.

Carol admitted that she had been spending more and more time in computer chat rooms. At first it was just for fun. Then she began enjoying the various people she was getting to know. Before long she began chatting almost exclusively with one man, Andrew. She was quick to say she would never leave her husband. This was just chat. And it really wasn't sexual in nature. Andrew just told her everything he was feeling. Carol felt as if she were dating Brett again.

Andrew, she said, was very "in touch with his emotions." He was divorced, because he loved his independence too much. This man was passionate, ambitious, but fragile too. "He's not afraid to tell me when he's hurting. I like that," said Carol.

Carol was in danger of falling for a guy she knew only from words typed on a screen. Her marriage had left her emotionally needy, and she was getting those needs met on-line. Apparently she had established certain boundaries for herself, but in time those could be erased. She might easily move into sexual chatting, fantasy, real-life meeting, and perhaps a physical affair. She was already conducting an emotional affair with Andrew.

But the counselor quickly recognized that everything Carol admired in Andrew was also there in Brett, only Brett was unable to verbalize it. And she herself was one reason that Brett couldn't express those feelings. She was listening well, responding well, and supporting well—but at her speed, not his. Even Andrew might clam up in a face-to-face encounter with her. The on-line relationship seemed to go so smoothly because Andrew had the time to deliver complete sentences and the freedom to exit whenever he wanted. Brett didn't have those luxuries in real life.

One of the remedies that the counselor suggested was that Brett send an e-mail to Carol each day. He could talk about anything, but it would be especially helpful if he would say how he felt about something. Carol could e-mail a response if she wanted, but she wasn't allowed to respond in real-life conversation. The counselor feared that, if she transferred those discussions to real life, she would dominate them again, and Brett would close up again. With e-mail, he had a safe environment in which to express his emotions.

Many couples are like this, unable to communicate at a meaningful emotional level. It's not that they don't care, just that they have different rhythms. Remember that women may have more connecting fibers in the brain. There's a superhighway running from their feelings to their tongues. Men have a dirt road along that route, with potholes and detours. Add to this the testosterone that makes men want to win every game. Since women have a huge head start in the emotion-expressing derby, most men would rather not even enter that race. So, like Brett, they close up.

In a situation like this, chat rooms can help and hurt. Frustrated wives like Carol find communicative friends on the net. But also they find men who seem more open than their husbands. On-line relationships can help fill the gap for these wives, providing the emotional connections they're not getting at home, but they can also lead a wife away from her marriage.

Of course it's not just wives who get led away by chat room relationships. Because husbands find that the rhythms and protections of Internet chatting allow them to open up in ways they don't in real life, they may enjoy the responsiveness of a female correspondent on-line. Men who get frustrated trying to express themselves to their wives suddenly have a chance to think about what they're saying before they say it. And they have the added security of anonymity and easy escape. For all we know, on-line "Andrew" could have been Brett.

Sex Chat

There's chatting and there's chatting. "I went shopping today" is a far cry from "I want to touch you all over." Some chat rooms promote tame conversations, while others are decidedly steamier. But in any chat room, once you pair off with someone, there's no telling what will be said. Many get involved in sex chatting, talking about the physical encounter they're imagining.

If you asked a group of men and a group of women whether sex chat constitutes cheating, we suspect the men would say no and the women would say yes. Both men and women participate in this fantasy world of on-line sex, but the women feel guiltier about it. Men are able to compartmentalize. Their computer fantasies are in a different cubicle of life. As long as they're not actually touching another woman, how could that be adultery? Women understand the power of emotional involvement. While they might come up with excuses for their on-line shenanigans, most wives sense that they're being unfaithful.

We keep hearing reports of women who never intended to get into sex chat but found their on-line relationships heading that way. We suspect this is something like the classic battle of teenage romance. That is, the guy pushes for sex while the girl wants intimacy. If he's shrewd, he'll learn to offer some intimate conversation to get the sex he wants. Meanwhile she learns to give in, at least a little, to his sexual demands to keep enjoying intimacy with him. As the saying goes, women use sex to get love, and men use love to get sex.

It wouldn't be surprising if the same pattern occurs in chat rooms—men pushing conversations toward increasing sexual content; and women, desperate for intimacy, going along. We don't mean to say that women don't enjoy sexual fantasy or that men don't seek intimacy. We just suspect that men tend to be the drivers in sexually explicit on-line relationships, and so some women who never sought sex chat to begin with find themselves moving toward it.

Pornography

It's no secret that men use pornography more than women. Studies have found that men are more visually stimulated. Men see a beautiful woman in a seductive pose and they get sexually charged. In Willard Harley's research on the needs of husbands and wives, men rated physical attractiveness third on the list of what they need from their wives. For women physical attractiveness didn't crack the top five. All of that explains why there's so much pressure on women in our society to be beautiful, while there's little pressure on men to be physically attractive.

Some men seek visual stimulation through pornography. They fantasize about the naked women they see pictured in magazines or videos—or, increasingly, on the Internet, which is essentially the largest pornography store you could ever imagine. A few women enjoy pornographic images of men, but their numbers are far fewer. Not only are men more apt to be visually stimulated, but several other distinctive male qualities feed into an addiction to pornography. If men are relationally challenged, pornography gives them a touch of sex without all that bothersome conversation. If men desire to control their relationships, that's easy when the object of their affection is merely an image on a screen. With on-line porn, men can have a new "relationship" every few seconds, if they choose (depending on how fast they can download images). In addition, men's ability to compartmentalize helps them to wall off this addiction in a secret corner of their otherwise normal lives.

Pornography is candy—sweet, pleasurable for a moment, but it can make you sick. It can also spoil your appetite. Who would choose broccoli over chocolate? But which is better for you? Truly nourishing relationships are sabotaged when one partner gets enticed by easy access to porn.

Other Uses of the Net

Research, stock quotes, fantasy sports, on-line computer games, shopping—there's a lot to do on the Internet. Men and women can avail themselves of these opportunities equally. These activities are generally harmless in themselves, but *any* activity can hurt a marriage when it becomes a preoccupation.

Tammy noticed a change in her husband soon after they upgraded their computer. John had longed for a state-of-the-art machine, and he and Tammy made it a mutual gift at Christmas. They also got a cable modem, signing up for high-speed Internet access. As a result, they could surf the net quickly, hitting many more web sites than they had before.

Though it belonged to both of them, the computer was mostly John's toy. He knew far more about it. He had taught Tammy some things, and she was catching on, but she still didn't know much beyond word processing.

Soon after they got the new computer, a pattern developed. John would get up from dinner, clear the dishes, and retreat to the den to "surf the net." He'd stay there most of the evening. Sometimes he'd be there quite late, coming to bed after Tammy was already asleep.

He was always very open about his Internet activities. Sometimes at dinner he'd tell her about a certain site he had visited. And she would often walk through the den while he was checking sports scores or playing on-line backgammon with a distant partner. So Tammy was rather confident that John wasn't exploring sex sites. But still she began to resent all the time he spent with the computer.

Many couples face a similar situation—one partner or the other getting involved in chat rooms or shopping on-line or just cruising the Information Superhighway. There's nothing wrong with doing that, but the time it takes can create tension in a marriage.

In *Men Are from Mars, Women Are from Venus*, John Gray talks about the "cave" that men often retreat to. Remember that men tend to be independent; they like to be in control; they are less savvy with language and relationships. So, as a protection, men often withdraw from participation with others and go into a kind of cave—to prepare, to heal, or just to relax.

That cave is often a specific place, like a den or study. Sometimes it's a particular time. In many homes, the whole family learns that they shouldn't bother Dad right after dinner or on Sunday afternoon. Maybe he camps out in the living room in front of the TV. You can sit with him, but don't try to talk. Maybe he goes out for a drive.

This withdrawal is necessary, as long as it's temporary. Wives need to respect the need for those private times, but they also need to coax their husband out of his cave when the appropriate time has been exceeded. It's not good for a relationship if the man shuts himself away for too long.

Now if the man's cave is equipped with a computer and a good modem, he could stay in there forever. Even if he's doing legitimate, innocent things, the exorbitant time spent apart from his wife will be damaging to the relationship.

Both men and women can be enticed away from a relationship by Internet activity. Men are more susceptible to pornography, and we feel women are somewhat more attracted to the relationships of chat rooms. Husbands and wives can both become preoccupied with otherwise innocent web pursuits, but we feel that the need many men have for "cave time" makes them especially prone to shut themselves away from their family, and the lure of the Internet can prolong this cave time to a dangerous degree.

Once again, we must admit that we're speaking in generalities. You and your spouse may relate to the Internet in ways that don't conform to these patterns. You need to talk together about your unique situation. But perhaps the tendencies we've mentioned will help explain why you do some of the things you do.

Information Please
Todd and Janet

Todd always considered himself to be an information junkie. From the time he was in college, he always felt the need to be informed at every level. General information and world news came from his constant listening to all-news stations. Though he couldn't afford regular subscriptions at the time, he devoured newspapers and political magazines whenever he could get his hands on them. Todd got his info "fix" from local libraries, professional offices, and even from trash cans.

The stock market also became a passion of his, even though he had no money to invest. It was a spectator sport for him, and he assembled an imaginary portfolio, gathering the daily closing numbers and earnings reports, then graphing them on charts by hand. This was the mid-1970s when that data was hard for the average person to get. Many times he would walk a mile from his college to visit a local stock brokerage firm and just sit and watch the ticker roll the information past his eager eyes.

Like many men, he also followed sports, especially when the local teams were doing well. He would track the scores, check the standings, and listen for the latest trade rumors as closely as he followed the stock market.

"Once," he says, "when our local baseball team was in a tight pennant race, I hooked up a transistor radio in my back pocket. The cord ran up through my shirt and I put the plug in my ear. That way, I could listen to games during classes. And I distinctly remember listening during a friend's wedding. This trick served me well for many years. I got updates on the stock market, sports scores, and late-breaking news reports, and only a small group of friends knew what I was up to. Some would seek me out when they wanted a score or something, but no one else seemed as interested as I was in the latest happenings from around the globe."

As Todd got older, his obsession with news never waned. Soon he had real money to invest, and even some extra cash to gamble on the teams he followed. Since he had followed the information trail for so long, he was convinced that he had a leg up on everyone else and was therefore destined to make his fortune by the time he was thirty. Now the need for information was even more important. It wasn't just a game anymore: His future depended on it. He would sneak away from work to call his broker or bookie—and of course neglected his job and his relationships to stay in touch with the latest happenings.

"I don't think anyone ever told me I was crazy or over the line or anything like that, but I also don't think anyone knew the half of what was really going on," he says. "Sure, I got comments on being distracted or aloof, but no one indicated that what I was doing was abnormal. That is, until I got married."

Todd married when he was twenty-five. His wife, Janet, was impressed with his wealth of knowledge and thought his stock market savvy would serve them well as they built their own nest egg. "Todd had goals and dreams," she says. "He knew what he wanted in life and had a plan on how he was going to get there. This impressed me, since all the other guys I dated seemed to be going nowhere. I saw Todd as someone who would be stable and successful, exactly what I thought I was looking for. Of course I never imagined the price I would pay for this image."

Janet went on to describe what life was like in the early years of their marriage. "Todd was not here for me. Sure, he came home at night, and, no, there was no mistress, but in one sense he had someone . . . no some*thing* else that was more important than me. It's hard to put your finger on, because it's not just one thing. It was a whole host of things, the newspaper, the TV, the ball game, the stock market; all of these *things* came before me. Todd would rush home from work—I thought to see me, but instead it was to turn on the TV to watch CNN or the business news. So I thought, *Okay, I'll give him time to unwind and then talk to him over dinner.* But many nights dinner included the TV on in the background or the newspaper or him opening his mail. It just went on and on."

Todd now realizes how "over the line" he was, and he admits it was not just on the home front. "My work was suffering too. I got access to cable TV at work. I found a way for the employees to all chip in so we could get it in the employee lounge, but really it was just me trying to find a way to track my investments during the day. I was taking more and more breaks and falling further and further behind in my work."

It all came to a screeching halt when Todd made a serious blunder in the stock market. His investing and, to a lesser degree, his gambling had grown increasingly risky until he invested everything on a stock that he thought was a sure bet. By this time, he wasn't telling Janet about his investments, because she'd been nagging him to slow down. She was even threatening to leave if he didn't stop following the stock market and start paying attention to her. Yet somehow Todd felt he could make it all up to her by winning big in the market.

"Well," he explains, "my sure bet went bankrupt and our entire nest egg was wiped out. I was devastated, and knew I had to tell Janet. After her initial anger, I was surprised about how understanding she was. I was clearly more upset than she was about the loss of our money and promised her that I would change. I knew that my whole life had to change, and I think Janet was really instrumental in my transformation. I stopped watching the stock market *completely* and stopped gambling on ball games. That was just the first step. Then I made certain commitments to Janet that she held me accountable for, things like not turning on the TV until after dinner or limiting my news watching to just one half-hour show per night. And most important I learned how to just relax—you know, sit on the back deck, sip coffee with Janet, and discuss our day. I think I had made some truly significant changes. And for a while our marriage and my life got much better."

That's when the Internet came along.

For an information junkie, the Internet represented the best high one could ever get. For Todd, it meant relapse. He began surfing the web the first time he got on-line. There was such a supply of information on stocks and sports and news, Todd was like a kid in a candy store.

He was fascinated by just about everything he found. Porn was not the problem for this Internet addict. Sure, he visited a few porn sites, just because they were there and he was curious, but they didn't do much for him. It was information he wanted. He'd be too busy looking up real estate prices in Canada or the price for flying overseas or the latest bid price on a Duncan yo-yo like the one he had when he was a kid. Todd was hooked.

At first Janet joined him in his curious search. They communicated with people overseas and planned exotic vacations that they would never take and chatted with people who had very strange lifestyles. But then, perhaps realizing that it was getting out of hand, Janet began to back away.

Todd sensed her disapproval and began to hide his time on-line from her. He started logging on at work, several times each day, and the same old danger emerged. He was neglecting his responsibilities on the job to feed his hunger for information. Only now he had a personal information machine right there on his desk. He also bought gadgets that would let him access information anywhere and anytime. This new capability gave him the confidence to get back into the stock market. Money had been tight for the family since his last investment fiasco, so the only money he could play with was their retirement fund. Appropriately, he invested in Internet stocks.

"I can't begin to tell you how thrilling it was to be back in the game," says Todd. "I could now set up my portfolio on the Internet and track my investment minute by minute. I could also monitor rumors about companies and earnings. I could even chat with people inside my favorite companies to get inside information about where these companies were headed."

But Todd's relapse went even further. His new access to information gave him the idea that he could gamble even more intelligently. Soon he was visiting casino web sites and sports-betting sites.

The whole time Janet was aware that something was very wrong, but she wasn't sure what. Her husband seemed distant from her. His energies were going in a different direction. For a while she thought he was having an affair, but that didn't add up. And it crossed her mind that maybe his old info-junkie days were back, but his habits at home—with TV, newspapers, even the computer—were all pretty normal. He was doing a very good job of hiding it.

Then disaster struck again. Internet stocks collapsed and so did Todd's investments. "It really scared me," he says. "The only comfort I could take in my own stupidity was the fact that many other investors suffered the same fate. Still, I knew I needed to tell Janet."

This time she was not nearly as gracious as she had been before. She didn't scream or scold; she just "clicked off," as she puts it. "I decided not to care anymore. If he wanted to run himself and his relationships into the ground again and again, let him. I had to be responsible for my own future." She began to make plans to move out. She had a good job and a group of supportive friends. She would just have to make it on her own.

Todd promised to see a counselor, and he begged Janet to go with him. Having been fooled by him twice, she wasn't sure whether to trust him, but she finally figured a counseling visit couldn't hurt.

The counselor got the full story from both partners and then concentrated on the time in the marriage when Todd's addiction was not a problem—after the previous disaster, when Janet forgave Todd and he temporarily changed his ways. "What was different about that time period?" the counselor asked.

The two began reminiscing about walks in the park, mornings on the deck, and deep conversations over dinner. "I remember not having to worry or hide my activities from her," Todd added.

"Why can't you do that again?" the counselor asked.

Janet shifted in her chair and crossed her arms in front of her. "It's too late to go back there. Todd can't change who he is."

The counselor looked back and forth at the two partners and then said slowly, "He doesn't have to change who he is; he just has to change. You both have to change some things. But the point is, Todd, you did it before, and you can do it again. Janet, you are the same person who forgave Todd and learned to love and respect him before. And, Todd, you are the same person who set proper boundaries and curtailed your obsession before. You know what you have to change. Now apply those same remedies to the present situation."

It sounds too easy, doesn't it? There's nothing easy about it. But often people feel weakened by an addiction—both the addicts and those who love them. The counselor was merely saying that they both had power to improve this situation.

Over the next several weeks, Todd and Janet met with the counselor and mapped out a plan for change. The assignments mostly concerned Todd's own personal discipline, but Janet had a few things to work on as well. As a result, Todd disconnected his Internet server for a year and put what little was left of his retirement money in a mutual fund that he then reviewed only once per quarter. "Most important," he says, "I went back to putting my energies into my relationship with Janet. We had to work at finding times to relax together, uninterrupted by any outside information. That sounds weird, to *work* at *relaxing*, but for an information junkie like me, that *is* work."

Now they get up an hour earlier to have coffee together and to plan their day. They schedule times together in the evenings to just talk. Sometimes they take walks in the park, and on days that they don't feel like talking, they watch a movie in bed together.

It's now a year since the latest crisis for Todd and Janet. "We have good weeks and bad weeks," Janet says, "but most of the time I believe our marriage is good. Surprisingly Todd's habits have truly changed. He watches the news most nights, but only for half an hour, and it's not that big a deal if he misses it."

"I have signed on to an Internet service again," Todd adds, "mostly for work-related or family e-mail, but I never really surf for information or allow myself to buy or research things on-line. I delete messages without reading them if they come from an unknown source and avoid anything that sounds like a stock tip or how I can make my fortune overnight."

Todd also tests himself from time to time by taking an e-mail holiday. He informs his family and friends that he won't be logging on for a while, and then he stays away from cyberspace entirely for about a week. "It's good if I find myself not being tempted to go on-line," he says. "It's even better that I dread logging on and finding lots of junk e-mail waiting for me—e-mail that all gets deleted without reading!"

And even better, he and Janet are still together and still in love.

four|

The Community

Sega222: Haven't seen you here in awhile.

Gollum: Yeah. Everything OK?

Trewbie2: I'm just stopping in to say goodbye.

Sega222: What's that supposed to mean?

Trewbie2: I'm not going to do chat rooms anymore.

Gollum: Is this some religious thing?

Sega222: You don't like us anymore? : (

Trewbie2: No. You're great. It was just getting crazy in my life. I was here all night. I couldn't stop.

Sega222: Hasn't bothered me. Last time I saw my husband was Christmas.

Gollum: 1992

Sega222: Ha ha

Trewbie2: Sorry. I'll miss you guys. But it's just something I have to do.

Gollum: How do you like that?

Sega222: Another one bites the dust.

Gollum: He'll be back. Ten bucks says he's back here in two weeks.

Sega222: You're on.

The Internet has always seen itself as a community, a group of people who occupy a new kind of geography—cyberspace. So let's take a look at that community. As with any city or town, different types of people spend their time there—rich and poor, moral and immoral, strong and weak. In real life, people live their lives with different motives, and the same is true on the Internet. Folks are driven by a desire for money, sex, and power, but also by more innocent longings for friendship, simple pleasure, or information.

When you interact with any members of this cyber-community on-line, it's as if you're inviting them into your home. Well, it's not quite as invasive as an actual home visit. You can wear your bathrobe if you want, and you don't have to serve tea and crumpets. But still, you are establishing a kind of relationship with a person, a merchant, an organization, or some other service on-line. Or your spouse is establishing such relationships. You always want to be careful about whom you invite into your home.

If the Internet is just a toy, you might not worry about the hours you or your spouse spend playing with it. But if you begin to see it as a "relationship machine," it takes on a whole new character. If your spouse is suddenly investing hours in a new relationship, that's something you should know about. It might be very innocent—a new pal at the gym, a potential business partner—but still, that new relationship must fit into *your* relationship. The same should be true about the Internet. And we're not just talking about chat rooms here. You or your spouse may have an on-line "relationship" with

ESPN or eBay or Yahoo or Playboy. Whatever kind of relationship that is, it must ultimately play second fiddle to your marriage relationship. If it doesn't, you're in trouble.

The Image Peddlers

In any community there are those who seek to use sex to make money. For reasons we've already mentioned—privacy, anonymity, speed—the web is highly conducive to the distribution of pornography, so it is found on the Internet in abundance. In 1997 one study found thirty-four thousand pornographic web sites. We expect that number has increased significantly with the ensuing explosion of the Internet.

Sites woo users with banner ads on other sites and with mass e-mailings. Traversing the Internet can be like walking through a red light district. If a man is susceptible to such temptations, it's very hard to say no.

Add to that the fact that nowadays pornography is seldom seen as a serious problem. Starlets who start web sites of their nude photos are hailed as enterprising businesswomen. Some compete to be "the world's most downloaded woman." Internet porn is joked about on talk shows and sitcoms. It's expected that any man with a healthy libido will check out some of those images. And isn't it safer for a man to look at pictures than actually to exchange fluids with a sex partner? Some consider pornography the ultimate safe sex.

But that's not a lot of comfort for Sarah, whose husband was channeling his libido into porn-inspired masturbation. Remember meeting Sarah and John at the beginning of this book? John was affectionate but showed no sexual desire for Sarah. It was a mystery—until she found him viewing computer porn one night.

73

Their story could be echoed by thousands of other couples. Pornography—on-line and otherwise—has hurt many marriages and destroyed some. It may seem like harmless fun to the comedy writers, but it has led many men into a fantasy world that they never really escape.

Let's look at this in terms of relationships. The porn user establishes a kind of relationship with the pornographic image, and that relationship may even progress through various stages. "I admire your beauty . . . I fantasize about being with you . . . I pleasure myself while I imagine being with you." Granted, some picture viewers stay at step one, aesthetically appreciating the beauty of a semiclad or unclad model. But most move on to fantasy, and many to masturbation. These stages of pornographic involvement can cause harm to a person's other (real-life) relationships.

At the fantasy level, the porn user goes swimming in a sea of lust. "I wish I could have this." But what is the object of this fantasy? A two-dimensional image of unrealistic proportions—perhaps impossibly beautiful, perhaps surgically sculpted. And after the makeup and lighting and airbrushing of photos, the models themselves don't look as good as their pictures.

So what's the harm in fantasizing about impossibly beautiful people? We think there are two major dangers. First, it raises the bar. Second, it destroys depth. It might be something like dreaming about winning the lottery. It's fun to fantasize about what you'd do with all that money, but then it gives you a pang of dissatisfaction when you look at your real-life bank account. The fantasy *raises the bar* to unrealistic levels, making it harder for real life to measure up. If a man spends hours gazing at young, gorgeous, well-built models (photographed with perfect lighting and makeup), and then climbs into bed with his real-life wife—how will he look at her? As Sarah said, she had no way of competing. The man who focuses his desires on unrealistic images is setting himself up for dissatisfaction when he leaves that fantasy world.

The second problem with pornographic fantasy is that it *destroys depth*. Try closing one eye as you drive. Well, maybe you'd better not. Our two-eyed vision gives us depth perception, which is very important to us as we get the whole picture of reality. Pornography is two-dimensional. (For the moment we're ignoring any new developments in virtual reality.) You observe an image on a screen and "what you see is what you get." It doesn't matter to you whether that person has a college education, keeps in touch with the family, worships God, or votes. You're fantasizing about a flat image. There is no depth perception, in any human, spiritual sense.

The problem occurs when you train your eyes to see this way. A man who spends hours looking at pornography can lose this kind of depth perception as he walks through life. He begins to see every woman in two dimensions, measuring her, stripping her, evaluating her—*what would she look like on that screen?* Feminists have long opposed pornography because it dehumanizes women. This is what they mean, not just that it reduces women to merely sexual beings, but that it squeezes the many dimensions of a woman's life into the flat surface of a screen or a page.

Baseball great Yogi Berra is credited with saying, "Ninety percent of this game is half mental." The same might be said of the sexual relationship between a husband and wife. It's not just about hormones, of course; there are major mental, emotional, and spiritual components as well. When one partner invests mental energy into pornographic fantasy, it robs the marital relationship of some sexual energy.

It gets even worse when the porn user takes the next step into masturbation. That's when the physical sexual energy gets sapped, as well as the mental energy. No wonder Sarah's husband, John, was perfectly content with hugs and cuddles. He was satisfying his hormonal drives in front of the computer screen. But that sexual energy rightly belonged to his wife. He was robbing her and investing the energy into a relationship with two-dimensional images.

One more thing about porn. You may be wondering why a guy like John would get into it, especially with a wife as fit and attractive as Sarah. Many wives face heartbreak over this very thing, worrying that they aren't beautiful enough, but it seldom has to do with that. More often it's a matter of communication and security. As relationships go, it's pretty easy to get along with an image on a screen. You don't have to "perform"; you don't have to worry about doing all the right things to please her; and you don't have to talk. For all these reasons, porn is an easy substitute for real relationships—especially for those men who have difficulty expressing themselves. One of the things wives can do in these cases is not necessarily make sex *better*, but make it *easier*, provide a sense of security and lowered expectations.

Talk of the Town

In our cybercommunity, there are chat rooms and other variations on that theme—newsgroups, bulletin boards, instant messaging, and so on. These are a mixed bag. As we've already seen, chat rooms can be the incubators for relationships that are good or bad. You can find a lifelong friend there or an illicit lover. As you stroll through this world, take note of the other folks strolling there. Are these good candidates for good friendships? If not, you may want to walk over to a different neighborhood.

The movie *The Breakfast Club* showed various high school kids in Saturday detention, and they each fit a particular stereotype—the brain, the nerd, the rebel, and so on. The fact is students do socialize in certain distinct groups, each with its own set of values and motives. If we were to do a *Breakfast Club* study of chat rooms, what groups would we find there? From our preliminary observation, we'll name four.

> *Connectors* just want to make friends. They get energized by the thought of socializing with other people around the world, and so they simply want to chat. Some of these connectors are single people in the market for a relationship, but they're not desperate. According to our definition, connectors have decent lives outside of cyberspace but simply use chat rooms as a healthy way to expand their world.
>
> *Needers* are desperate connectors. They generally have trouble relating to others in the real world, and so they go on-line to have their social needs met. Often they have poor self-esteem, and this can lead them to a poor sense of boundaries. If they're single (or in unsatisfying marriages), they may seek potential mates on the web, but their standards are usually quite low, and they often find themselves in conversations that have moved out of their comfort zone.
>
> *Predators* prowl the chat rooms looking to take advantage of others. Maybe they're just there for kicks, or maybe they have worse motives. Some push innocent chat toward sexual subjects, and some seek to follow up computer chat with personal

meetings. Some predators seek personal information that could be used later for credit card fraud or the like. Some sexual predators invade teen chat rooms to see what mischief they can find there.

Wanna-bes use chat rooms as a make-believe world. They experiment with different identities and try to pass themselves off as the real deal. Some men masquerade as women or vice versa. Some adults pretend to be children. Some present themselves as having a different job or a different background. By our definition, the wanna-be isn't trying to prey on anyone. He or she just wants to be someone else for a while.

Connectors are, of course, the healthiest in these groups. There is still a chance that these people could become preoccupied and throw their lives out of balance by spending too much time in chat rooms, but generally their motives are good. Connectors need to be wary of the predators, establish healthy boundaries with the needers, and always remember that an on-line pal may turn out to be someone quite different than represented.

Needers are especially susceptible to Internet addiction. They should set up strict limits on Internet use, so they don't neglect their real-life issues. If they can establish good relationships on-line with wise boundaries, great! But they must be very careful about the predators. Predators eat needers for lunch.

Wanna-bes can also create unintended damage by leading on a needer. A playful "let's pretend" relationship on-line can raise unrealistic hopes in a needer. It's a sad day when a middle-aged woman learns that the wealthy businessman who's been wooing her on-line each evening is actually a fourteen-year-old girl. In general, needers must realize that they won't get their needs met on-line. The Internet can be a nice place to visit, but they shouldn't live there. They should seek to build healthy, whole lives in their real world, with Internet use being only a part of that.

Predators can cause great damage to everyone else on the net. The worst of them are criminal. Others may just be looking for sexual thrills by turning innocent conversation into smut. If you find yourself veering in this direction, stop. Get off-line. Get help. Get an appointment with a counselor as soon as possible.

Wanna-bes also play a dangerous game. For them, a chat room is just a masquerade party, but they forget that connectors and needers are trying to form real friendships. Wanna-bes should be careful about leading any on-line relationship too far before the mask is removed.

One of the people we interviewed for this book told us about his concern for his teenage daughter, who was following the example of her mother and getting involved in sex chat on-line. With pain in his voice, he told how the girl crept out to meet some guy in a hotel and then came home in tears, saying he had raped her. Of course the father pressed charges, and the authorities were prosecuting the man for statutory rape of a minor—until he showed them the e-mails in which the girl had claimed to be eighteen. In this case the masquerade turned out to be a dangerous game.

You may be entering chat rooms seeking innocent diversions or honest relationships but be careful. You may encounter those who want to use you, those who want to fool you, and those who want to hurt you.

There are different kinds of chat rooms, of course, and you can learn to take the temperature of a room pretty quickly. Some rooms seem to encourage racy conversation, and others don't. If you're looking to make new friends, one commonsense rule applies: Go where there are people you want to meet. This makes sense in real life as well as in cyberspace. We always marvel at how single people say they want to find responsible, faithful, spiritual partners, and where do they go to find such partners? Bars. On the Internet you need to concentrate your involvement in the places where you find kindred spirits. If you're looking for relationships— romantic or platonic—with people who are intellectual, creative, spiritual, or compassionate, look for those chat rooms that specialize in that kind of chat.

There will always be predators and wanna-bes lurking around, even in the best sites, and needers are prevalent. But if you set good boundaries and stay alert, you'll be able to grab the best from Internet connections and avoid the dangers.

When It's a Problem

As we've seen, pornography is inherently destructive to a marriage, and chat rooms can lead a spouse astray. And then there are all the other Internet pursuits that have no built-in dangers, but they can still become problematic.

Remember Todd, who described himself as an "information junkie"? What could be wrong about checking stock prices or getting an update on a baseball score? Nothing at all, unless it starts stealing you away from your marriage. If it becomes an obsession, you need to control it. If it becomes a convenient escape—which lets you avoid the real-life issues of marriage building—you have to make a concerted effort to pull yourself away from the computer and refocus on your spouse. It may not be a pornographic image you're looking at, but it could be just as damaging if it draws you away from quality time with your wife. It may not be a secret lover you're e-mailing every night, but if that activity draws you away from your husband, it's nearly as bad.

How do you know when your Internet use is going too far? Consider the three Ss. Are you *sneaking* around? Is it *sidetracking* your attention? Is it *sapping* your energy?

Sneaking Around

Sometimes in a counseling session, Tom will hear a client say, "My wife doesn't know this, but . . ." Whatever the next phrase is, it's trouble. It might be something rather innocent: "I'm looking for a new job"; "I still have a cigarette now and then"; "I got a speeding ticket last week." That doesn't matter. If it's important enough to tell a counselor, but it's being hidden from a spouse, that means there's something wrong with the marriage.

Sometimes it just means that the other spouse is a nag, but that still identifies a marital problem. There is a lack of communication, a lack of openness, a lack of safety.

As his Internet addiction grew, Todd was living a lie. He used his office computer to seek out the information he needed, just so his wife wouldn't know how much time he was spending on-line. No doubt, he rationalized all this. "What she doesn't know won't hurt her." Well, it did hurt her when he lost their life savings in a bad investment.

If you are trying to hide the extent of your Internet use from your spouse, you have a problem. *Perhaps* it's merely a problem of communication. *Perhaps* you just need to talk openly about how much you need to go on-line, and then you can reach an agreement on an appropriate number of hours. But it's more likely that you're hooked, and you don't want your spouse challenging you. In any case, you have to stop sneaking and start talking.

Marriage brings built-in accountability. Your life is so intertwined with that of your spouse that you each have a right to know what's going on in the other's life. You *must* answer to one another. Certainly this can lead to problems of nagging and controlling behavior, but if it's handled in a healthy way, it can give each partner a much needed outside perspective on life.

Sidetracking Attention

Is your Internet use sidetracking your attention? Are you distracted in your daily life by thoughts of what you'll do the next time you're on-line? When you're with your family, or alone with your spouse, are you not all there, because you're envisioning your next Internet voyage? Has your work suffered? Have your conversations been dominated by web matters? Have you forgotten or ignored important information related to you by your spouse or children, because your mind was elsewhere?

For Scott it was fantasy baseball. Each spring he drafted a team of real-life baseball players, and a web site totaled the statistics of those players week by week throughout the season. He competed with a dozen good friends who had drafted their own teams. All in good fun, right? But Scott began to think about his fantasy team *all the time*. In the weeks before the annual draft, he didn't get much work done, because he kept planning his strategy and rechecking the stats of the available players.

Every night he went on-line to track the play-by-play of eight different National League ball games. He visited three different sports sites to get the latest info on players' injuries and exciting new rookies. When he saw his buddies, their conversation invariably turned, not only to sports, but to their fantasy teams. They weren't always sure who was in first place in the real standings, but they knew that Scott's shortstop stole three bases and scored twice on the previous night.

Scott's wife, Beth, shrugged it off at first. Boys will be boys. But soon she realized that this wasn't just a healthy interest in sports; this was an obsession. Since Scott had a sales job and worked on commission, she saw the change in their income when baseball season was about to start. She knew she'd have no quality time with him in the evenings between April and October. She came to recognize the faraway look in his eyes at dinner. And she learned quickly that, when they got together with his pals, she'd be totally left out of their conversation.

She kept telling herself that it could be worse. Scott could be taking gambling trips to Atlantic City or visiting strip clubs, but it still bothered her. She desperately wanted him to pay more attention to her—and not just in the off-season.

There's a line in Arthur Miller's great play *Death of a Salesman*. The wife says, "Attention must be paid." She's chastising her grown sons for ignoring the decline of their father, but we could borrow that wonderful line as a prescription for any good marriage. Attention must be paid. In the traditional marriage vows, the bride and groom promise to honor each other. That means paying attention to your partner, listening, responding. If your Internet involvement is preventing you from doing that, you need to make some major changes. Attention must be paid.

Sapping Energy

Nighttime was the danger zone for Carolyn. Her husband, Al, was an "early to bed, early to rise" guy, and she never got into that schedule. She did freelance editing work at home, so she could be there when the kids got in from school in the afternoon. Of course Al had to get them out to the school bus in the morning. This arrangement worked well for them. Evenings after dinner were good family time, and Al and Carolyn usually found some time to be alone with each other on weekends.

But then they got their computer modem, and Carolyn began surfing the net late at night. She never got into the chat rooms much. In fact sometimes she was actually doing important research for her editing work. But mostly she was just cruising, looking at all the interesting sites, until four or five in the morning.

Al was such a sound sleeper, he never noticed, but she often crawled into bed about a half hour before he awoke. That meant she slept for most of the morning, but still felt groggy when she got up. Then there was only an hour or two before the kids got home. Her editing work began to suffer. Jobs she used to turn around in two weeks were taking two months. She'd yell at the kids for distracting her, and she always felt too tired to do much housework. Her fatigue even affected their sex life. She lacked the energy to do much except cuddle.

Amazingly it took a while before she realized what was going on. Al suggested that she see a doctor. He had read about chronic fatigue syndrome—maybe that was her problem. But then he woke up one morning to find her still at the computer. Though she had been up all night, she displayed an energy he hadn't seen for quite some time.

"Working on some deadline?" he asked.

"No, just surfing."

"It's 6 A.M., Carolyn."

"You know me," she shrugged. "I'm a night owl."

"Well, I wish you pushed *my* buttons like that."

That got her thinking. She didn't sleep well that morning, and throughout the next day, she took stock of her life. She saw how her rampant Internet use was robbing hours from her family. She was pouring so much energy into the computer, she had little left for them. She made the decision to set some rules for herself. She wouldn't let the Internet take over her life like that.

Marriage takes work. Besides the basic effort of maintaining a household, a husband and wife need to serve each other. This requires energy, whether it's making a bed or making love. When one partner's energy is sapped, for whatever reason, the relationship suffers.

As we've seen in numerous examples, the Internet can be a black hole sucking time, energy, and attention out of your life. There's a funny commercial in which a web user hears the announcement, "You have reached the end of the Internet." It's funny because it could never happen. This ocean is so vast, we could surf it forever.

The Internet is a helpful servant. It can save you time as you seek information. But if you let it become your master, it will steal time from you. It will take over your life if you let it.

Hole to Whole

Any addiction or obsession involves an effort to fill a hole in our life. Some experts talk about wounds that we're trying to salve. We feel needy, and somehow we get the idea that this *thing* will meet our need. The *thing* might be alcohol or drugs. Maybe it's the thrill of gambling big money on the roll of dice. Maybe it's the temporary distraction of shopping or working or surfing the Internet.

Many of us have these holes in our soul, and we reach out for a variety of "fixes." Some are dangerous and physically addictive. Others are merely behavioral distractions. We're not saying that Internet use is a drug, but we are saying that it can become an obsession, as people try to find wholeness on-line and, ironically, alter their lives and relationships in unhealthy ways.

We don't become whole with quick fixes. Wholeness takes time. It involves discipline and order and restraint and balance. It requires good relationships. Don't let Internet obsession rob you of the wholeness for which you long.

The Catalyst
Gail and Jim
Andy and Karen

The odd thing was Gail always seemed somewhat antisocial. At least that's what her husband, Jim, thought. She didn't have a lot of friends. He was always taking the lead when it came to going out with others, attending parties, or even keeping in touch with relatives. She would just as soon stay home, spending time with Jim and their young son, Danny.

It was Jim who introduced her to computers in general, and on-line communication in particular. The computers at the library had access to message boards, and Jim thought it was fun to connect with people around the world. He showed Gail how to do this, and she got hooked.

Jim soon tired of the message boards, but Gail kept going back to the library—until they got a computer of their own. Then Gail spent hours instant messaging with friends everywhere. It had always been a struggle to get Gail out of the house to do anything social, but now it was impossible. She was meeting her social needs on-line. Increasingly Jim felt squeezed out of the picture.

For the longest time, the whole thing seemed innocent. The Internet was a plaything. Jim and Gail would joke about the time she spent on-line, and she would tell him about the interesting people she met there. It was just a phase, Jim assumed. It would pass.

Saying that she wanted to care for little Danny, Gail quit her job. But that just meant she could be on the Internet more. Danny was attending half days of kindergarten, but Jim learned that he was often late or absent. Gail would stay up with the computer all night and then be too exhausted to get Danny to kindergarten or care for him properly.

Gail became especially active in chat rooms catering to teenagers. She was twenty-eight, but her on-line pals were thirteen, fourteen, and fifteen. They seemed fascinated by her grown-up life, and she invented stories to keep them interested. She became much more open sexually.

She would talk about anything and everything, which of course her adolescent cyberpals were eager to hear. Jim suspects she even engaged in cybersex conversations with some of these minors.

When Jim finally confronted Gail about his concerns, she was defiant. He was no longer the most important part of her life, she announced; the Internet was.

Then she left. Seven years into their marriage, Jim and Gail separated. He received custody of Danny. They haven't spoken in a year. He's not sure where she is.

"I believe we would have had problems in our marriage eventually," Jim says. "The Internet just served as the tool to make it happen."

As we did research for this book, we expected to find many stories of men seduced by on-line pornography. What surprised us was the number of stories like this one about Jim and Gail. Men aren't the only ones succumbing to the lure of the Internet. A substantial number of women are getting tangled up in the web as well, drawn away from their real-life relationships.

The pattern is eerily similar. The computer enters the home for wholesome reasons. Often it's even the husband who introduces his wife to the Internet. In many of these cases, the husband tries the chat rooms but gets bored by them, even as the wife is growing more enchanted. It seems like an innocent hobby at first, but eventually the wife begins spending her life on-line. Real-life friendships dwindle as social needs are met in cyberspace. Internet use soon occupies all the free hours between work and sleep and other obligations. Then it starts robbing hours from those other obligations, from work, and even from sleep. "Staying on-line all night" is a common refrain. "Quitting her job to stay home" is another. Family needs are ignored and the marriage bed is avoided. Frequently the wife finds a "special man" on-line and begins a relationship, which escalates into cybersex and sometimes to long phone calls and real-life meetings. Often the wife leaves her husband for this other man. But even when there's no specific other man, there's a virtual separation in the marriage. Husband and wife have lost intimacy. The wife is basically married to the computer.

Andy was madly in love with his wife, Karen. When her parents moved halfway across the country, Karen wanted to move too, just to stay close to them. Andy was happy to oblige, even though it meant uprooting his career.

Married for six years by this time, they were both nearing thirty. But Karen had never really *found herself*, to use the modern lingo. Uprooting wasn't hard for her, since she had never been at a job for very long. Every couple of years, she hatched a new career plan that would finally bring her fulfillment. Andy went along for the ride—anything to keep her happy.

After their move, Karen had a new plan. She would go into church work, perhaps even becoming a minister in their Methodist denomination. What could be more fulfilling than that? They couldn't afford seminary tuition at the time, but she could start by taking some basic courses on-line. That meant she wouldn't have to look for a new job, since she'd be focusing on her classes, but she'd be home to look after their three-year-old daughter. Oh, yes, and they would definitely need to buy a computer.

It took three days, Andy says, for Karen to get into the sex web sites. Then she entered the sex chat rooms. A week later she had a phone conversation with someone she met on-line. Soon she was spending ten to twelve hours a day on the Internet. Andy warned her that this was becoming a problem, and he urged her to get rid of the computer. No way, she replied. It was under control. Checking the cache files, he learned what chat rooms she visited. So during the day at work, he'd log into the same sites to see what she was saying. He was appalled. Again he insisted that she get rid of the computer. Again she refused. They began to talk about separating.

Then Karen met a man on-line. Within a month they arranged a rendezvous. She wasn't even secretive about it. Andy filed for divorce and won custody of their little girl. Karen moved to L.A. with her cyberlover, but moved back in with her parents a year later.

There's that pattern again. Another marriage bites the dust. Jim and Andy are both understandably bitter about the Internet and the trouble it caused them, but did the Internet really cause these breakups? Yes and no.

Andy and Karen were in trouble before they even saw a computer. Their relationship was built on infatuation and convenience; it was classically one-sided. Andy calls Karen "self-centered," but he enabled her to be that way. She apparently felt a deep need for "fulfillment," and she sought it in various forms and was regularly disappointed.

Were they doomed then from the start? Not necessarily. Yes, there are thousands of unbalanced marriages like that, which totter for six or seven years before they finally topple. But good counseling early in the process might have helped them deal with the unhealthy patterns in their marriage. And that might have lessened the impact of the Internet.

As it was, the web wasn't so much the cause of their problems as the catalyst. Karen was a "fulfillment junkie," and the Internet specializes in promises of fulfillment. Remember that she initially planned to take seminary courses on-line. So the Internet was offering her a way to find fulfillment serving God—without all that fuss of actually attending classes. Very quickly, the nature of that fulfillment shifted gears as she began to seek fulfilling relationships without all the fuss of, say, going to a singles bar.

In the case of Jim and Gail, the danger wasn't as obvious. But Gail seems to be a different sort, a late bloomer. Remember that she seemed somewhat antisocial, according to her husband. There may have been some sort of phobia that kept her from enjoying social interactions—except on-line. Apparently she felt much freer with her Internet friends, and this led to a blossoming of sorts. Anonymous at her computer, she was released from the fears that had always held her back. Suddenly she was relating to a broad community of people, and loving it. It's interesting that she hung out with teenagers, because in many ways she was going through another adolescence herself. She was discovering herself socially in a way that many teenagers do.

This sort of thing happens with both women and men, and it doesn't always involve the Internet. Husbands and wives change through time. They grow in various ways, good and bad. We're all familiar with the classic midlife crisis in which the successful executive pierces his ears and buys a red sports car. He's a new man, he says, which leaves his wife stymied. "I preferred the man I married," she says.

But there's another "early marriage crisis" in which a husband and wife realize they're both continuing to grow. After a few years of building a life together, they turn their attentions back to their personal lives. Sometimes they start feeling that the marriage is holding them back. This typically happens in years five to ten of a marriage. It's that storied "seven-year itch," except it's not just about boredom or restlessness. It's a matter of personal growth.

The challenge for any couple in those danger years is to work together to support the personal growth of both spouses. To put it in terms of simple pronouns: In the early years of a marriage, the *I* is neglected as both partners forge a powerful *we,* but then the *I* comes storming back. This can destroy the marriage, unless the couple can find a way to let the *we* strengthen both *I*'s.

Gail was finding herself on the Internet. She had happily sublimated her *I* to the *we* of her marriage, but now she was exhilarated with the new possibilities of social interaction on the Internet. Would the problems have happened without the net? Maybe sometime, somehow. But the Internet was a powerful catalyst for Gail's transformation. The real problem, however, was that her personal growth led her away from the marriage. She wanted to explore what the new Gail could do elsewhere.

Many readers of this book will see themselves in the middle of these stories, or earlier stories we've told. Maybe the separation hasn't occurred yet, but you're in danger. Maybe the pattern is beginning to emerge. Maybe your innocent hobby is taking up more and more time. Maybe your spouse stayed up all night last night surfing the net.

We're not saying the Internet is evil, but it does exploit weaknesses. It could be the catalyst that takes the weaknesses of your marriage and ratchets them up to a new level. You need to take bold action to strengthen your marriage. See a counselor. Spend good time together. Even surf the net together. Maybe it's not too late.

```
five[
```

Craving
Entertainment

Rich223: What's up?

Flutterby: Nothing much.

Rich223: Me neither.

Flutterby: I'm just so bored here. Boring job. Boring marriage. Boring life.

Rich223: I know what you mean.

Flutterby: Where would we be without our net pals?

Rich223: Bored.

Flutterby: You said it.

Rich223: Sure did.

Flutterby: So what's up?

Rich223: Nothing much.

Flutterby: Me neither.

What on earth did people do for fun before the Internet came along? What did they do before TV, before radio, before electric lights stretched day into evening?

Oh, they had pleasant times, to be sure. There have always been community events and festivals. Music, dance, and theater have long been part of the human experience. But we've never had so much of it. Today our entertainment options are overwhelming. If a time traveler visited the twenty-first century from the eighteenth, he or she would go crazy trying to keep up with all the sensory stimulation we take for granted. If we were to go back a century or two, we'd be incredibly bored.

Perhaps you're old enough to remember the days before TV became commonplace. Families would gather at night and watch the radio. Seriously! Nowadays radio is something to listen to while doing something else, but then it was the only game in town.

Or maybe you grew up with three TV channels. Or, if you weren't in a metropolitan area, just one or two—and fuzzy reception at that. If you held the antenna and stood on one foot, you could see a faint image of Dick Van Dyke tripping over the footstool. We remember that it was a big deal to get a UHF converter for the TV set. Suddenly our channel options doubled.

Now how many channels do you have? Cable companies are offering three hundred, and still people complain that there's nothing on. It's not uncommon for us to crash in front of the TV, remote control in hand, and click through all those channels without finding anything worth watching. Our visitor from the eighteenth century would be fascinated by the emergency broadcast signal! Obviously we're spoiled.

And that's just television. We haven't even talked about the Internet yet. If cable TV has expanded our entertainment options a hundredfold, the Internet makes that increase exponential. The net can bring you TV and radio from around the globe, as well as a huge catalogue of movies and music. And we've already discussed the vast array of information, images, and chat groups available. We have at our fingertips virtually any kind of entertainment imaginable—and still we want more. Here we are. Now entertain us!

As a culture, we are addicted to entertainment. Writer Neil Postman made the point brilliantly in his book *Amusing Ourselves to Death*. The worst thing for us is to be bored. We constantly seek sensory stimulation. In fact a new generation has grown up adept at multitasking. We used to blame *Sesame Street* and MTV for the rapid succession of images that shrank the previous generation's attention span. But now you'll see a kid watching TV while listening to a Walkman, playing a Game Boy, and talking on a cell phone. And somehow never missing a beat.

No question about it. Our world is for thrill seekers, and the technology of entertainment has raised the bar to impossible levels. The more stimulation we get, the more we crave. Entertainment is a drug; we can never get enough. We might feel sated for a short time, but soon we're back with a thirst for more—and the Internet is more than ready to supply these needs. We're only limited by our own capacity to partake of it.

This is the world in which you're trying to salvage a marriage. If you or your spouse is dealing with an Internet addiction of some sort, it's not all that surprising. In this world we are trained to be entertainment addicts, from Bert and Ernie to Will and Grace. So is it any wonder when this incredible machine—the computer—pushes us over the edge?

Why are we saying this? Because many treat Internet addiction as a rare disease. People are ashamed to confess when they have a problem with it, and spouses are hesitant to admit that they're married to someone who does. Of course denial is a major component of any continuing addiction, and denial is often held in place by guilt.

But the fact is that Internet addiction is not rare at all. In a world that celebrates "entertainment addiction" in general, it's certainly understandable that some would let their fascination with the vast resources of the net get out of control. While we can understand it, we don't excuse it. Certainly this fascination has led some to do shameful things—neglecting family, carrying on affairs, or indulging in pornographic perversity—but at least we can see how they got to that point. Shameful deeds bring feelings of shame, and they should. But we can let those guilty feelings motivate us to confess, get help, and undo the damage.

Meanwhile spouses should understand that we're dealing with a sickness of our entire culture. Your addicted spouse is merely going with the flow. Going *too far* with that flow, no doubt, but you do need to recognize that our world is rife with temptation. To find renewed health for your marriage, you're going to need to go *against* the flow. Together, you'll need to challenge the entertainment addiction that everyone else takes for granted.

Blessed Boredom

As he retired from an illustrious career, baseball player Tony Gwynn was asked why he was such a great hitter. "Because I'm boring," he replied, explaining that good hitting requires doing the same thing the same way every time, day in, day out. "Even my wife and kids say I'm boring," he laughed. But in his career he stepped up to the plate more than ten thousand times, did the same old thing each time, and rapped out more than three thousand hits, for a batting average better than anyone else's in his era.

You could say the same thing about marriage. People keep thinking they want more excitement in their marriage, but honestly, marriages grow strongest in their boring times. You're looking at ten thousand, maybe fifteen or twenty thousand mornings of waking up next to the same person. Day in, day out, the same things will happen. Yes, there will be new challenges, and both partners will continue to grow, but if you're going to make it through, you'll have to make peace with the ennui of marriage. Marriage is *supposed* to be boring, at least some of the time.

Don't get us wrong. Husbands and wives should continually look for new ways to express their love for each other, and this can become very exciting. But we're talking about 24/7 here. If you demand nonstop excitement every hour, even the excitement will get boring. We have seen marriages get into serious trouble because of the fear of boredom. Worried that something's missing from their relationship, or that the magic has died out, some husbands and wives try all sorts of crazy tactics to "rekindle the fire." What they mean is that they think their marriage should be more entertaining.

So they try kinky sex techniques, sometimes even using pornography or other partners. They get cosmetic surgery or go on exotic vacations or buy new cars or wardrobes. Ultimately they stop being themselves. They're frantically trying to entertain each other, but they end up scuttling the very thing that brought them together in the first place—their simple love for one another.

The problem is there isn't really a problem. Husbands and wives don't have to entertain each other. That's not in the job description. Love and cherish, yes. Be there in sickness and health, absolutely. But dancing the Macarena in the nude while twirling sparklers? Not necessary.

When we buy into the entertainment addiction of our culture, we demand to be dazzled in every aspect of life. People quit boring jobs so they can "follow their bliss." And people quit boring marriages when a more entertaining prospect comes along. But it shouldn't be like that. Excitement is not a basic human need; love is. Far too many people these days ditch lasting love for momentary excitement. Don't let that happen to you.

Every marriage is boring, at least some of the time. That doesn't mean anything is wrong. It just means life is being lived, consistently, day in, day out, like Tony Gwynn swinging at a baseball. Don't let the entertainment culture force you out of your game. Be yourself in your marriage. Love creatively, with your whole self, but be true to who you are. As you grow, you and your partner will mesh in different ways, like the turning shapes of a kaleidoscope, but you don't need to force the issue with radical alterations. For entertainment value, you'll never be able to compete with MTV and its new image every 2.4 seconds or with stand-up comics or hot looking stars or for that matter with the Internet and its vast collection of data, images, and people. But you've got something far more valuable on your side. You've got love.

The Addiction Machine

If you were trying to create a machine that would make people addicted to it, how would you design it? Well, it would need to dispense something that people need or at least that they *think* they need, like social status, escape, peace of mind, or—how about this?—entertainment. You would need to create instant gratification so that the user merely has to push a button and the benefits are provided. You would need to offer small doses, but promise huge satisfaction, and try to make it so that the user has to use it more and more to achieve the desired effect. And of course it would be extremely helpful if the addictive machine could be used in the privacy of one's own home, perhaps in a closed-off room, where no one would have to know the extent of a person's use.

Oops! Apparently that machine has already been invented.

We have already discussed the ways in which the anonymity, privacy, and easy access of the Internet make it an ideal conduit for pornography and prurient chat. We don't need to rehash that here, but we do want to expand the discussion. If our culture is addicted to entertainment—and by that term we mean the rapid onslaught of new sensory stimulation—then the Internet is the ultimate addiction machine. It can dish out the entertainment as fast as we can receive it. And the stimulation can take as many different forms as we desire. Dirty pictures? Got 'em. Racy conversation? Got plenty of that. And if you just want to download stock quotes or sports scores, go wild. The info autobahn is humming away, and you can hitch a ride any time you like. Now let's put all of these observations together.

Our culture is addicted to entertainment—new stimuli. We can easily be swept along with that tide. In fact, because of the available onslaught of excitement, we're tempted to think that our marriages aren't exciting enough. As a result we either try drastic (and usually doomed) methods to rekindle excitement in our marriage or allow our attention to drift away from our marital relationship into other, more exciting pursuits. And, hey, look at that! There's an entertainment machine right there in your home! Well, actually you have several. The TV's been there for a while, but when you can't find anything good on its three hundred channels, try the three million channels of the Internet. If you're drifting away from your boring spouse, why not drift over to the den and spend all your free time surfing?

Fighting Back

That's what we're dealing with. Internet addiction isn't just a bad habit, like biting your nails. It's a cultural crisis. If it is troubling your marriage, you need to make fundamental changes in how you think about marriage and about entertainment. We have three suggestions for fighting back: Take a break from all the entertainment stimuli in which you normally indulge, work on enhancing your marriage, and learn how to tame the Internet. Your neighbors may think you're a little odd, but they're not the ones you're fighting for.

Take a Break

Every February millions of Christians decide to give up something for Lent. Some use this season as a time of self-improvement. For example, they go on a diet or try to quit smoking. But that's not really the point. The point of giving something up for Lent is to demonstrate that everything else pales in importance when compared to your relationship with the Lord. You don't just give up bad things for Lent; you can give up *anything*, just to show that God has first place in your life.

We're suggesting the same sort of tactic in challenging the entertainment addiction of our culture. We're not saying that all entertainment is evil, just that you may want to take a break from it for a while. Do you watch TV every evening? Do you always have music playing? Do you go to a show every weekend? Are you surfing the web every night? Whatever your entertainment "drug of choice" is, why not cut back for a time? Try to enjoy a less exciting life.

That might sound like a contradiction—how can you enjoy it if it's less exciting?—but that's the whole idea. Rediscover simple pleasures. Go for a walk with your spouse. Share back rubs. Talk. You don't need some electronic appliance tossing grenades at your senses to find fulfillment. Slow down a bit and treasure simplicity.

You can choose your own strategy, depending on how serious your entertainment addiction is. If you think you can't possibly do without all your tunes, shows, and web sites, it's even more important that you find a way to turn it all off for a while. Take some down time. You can "fast" from these things for a day, a week, or a Lenten-type season.

But it's not just about turning things off; it's about turning yourself on to low-key delights. Watch the sun set some evening. Make friends with a goldfish. Color with your kids. Read. Hike. Play Monopoly. Sing folk songs with your family or your neighbors.

Embrace Your Marriage

The second tactic for fighting back is to embrace your marriage. We mean two things by this. First, accept the fact that your marriage won't always be deliriously exciting. As we've said, sometimes marriage is boring and that's okay. The second point is that you should invest yourself fully in this relationship. Your renewed investment in your marriage may inject new life into it.

Probably you remember the dating process as an exciting time of mutual discovery. The wedding itself is usually a memorable event, and the honeymoon exquisite. Even the first year or so of marriage is full of newness for the young couple. Then it quickly gets old.

All sorts of uncomfortable feelings emerge during the time of disillusionment that follows the initial exciting years. Partners can begin to resent each other for not being quite as exciting anymore. They may worry that they've sacrificed their individual hopes and dreams for an unsatisfying relationship. Of course this is hard to talk about, so the feelings often remain hidden, where they can fester for years. A husband and wife sometimes turn away from each other during this time—sometimes literally, in bed or on the couch, but certainly in a figurative sense. They begin to hedge their bets by investing less in the relationship and more in themselves. So guess what? The relationship loses passion and becomes even less exciting.

At this point you must do more than just buy new lingerie. Various attempts to liven up your marriage may work briefly, but there's a deeper issue. Both husband and wife need to recommit to the marriage, embracing the idea that it will have both exciting times and mundane times. In a way you need to go back to those marriage vows, pledging your love "for richer, for poorer, in sickness and health, *when brilliant and when boring."* Resist our culture's overemphasis on entertainment. Your marriage can be fun sometimes, but stop being disappointed with your spouse for not providing a nonstop three-ring circus.

This is one of those bits of advice that's easy to read in a book but hard to put into practice—not that it's complicated; it's just gutsy. You have to make a decision every day to *be married to this person.* Turn *toward* your spouse—physically and figuratively. Stop looking for the exit sign and commit yourself for the long haul, which will include days both boring and blessed.

In his counseling practice, Tom has often heard one spouse throwing the blame on the other. "I'm having an affair because he never listens to me." "I shut down emotionally because she doesn't understand me." Increasingly he hears statements like this: "I spend all my time on-line because my spouse doesn't excite me anymore."

Whose fault is that? Notice how the person puts the responsibility on the spouse to provide excitement. Supposedly, if that basic need isn't met, it's grounds for withdrawal. But that's a warped view of marriage. It's a warped view of humanity.

You have no basic right to entertainment. You do have a basic responsibility to love your spouse. Boredom is no excuse for abandonment. Turn off your computer and go embrace your spouse. Embrace your marriage, with all its faults and tedium, with all its wonders and pleasures.

Tame the Net

We'll talk more later about how to tame the net, but for now we'll just discuss its importance. If our culture pushes entertainment addiction, and if that makes us despise our marriage for being boring, then the Internet has an easy job of feeding our addiction and destroying our marriage. We can try to curtail the addiction by simplifying our lives and avoiding the brainwashing of the entertainment culture. We can embrace our marriage, even though it's not always as thrilling as that tractor pull on ESPN2. But we also need to see the Internet as the voracious creature it is and find a way to tame its influence in our lives.

Imagine that a man finds a baby bear in the woods. It's so cute that he has to bring it home to his family. And so the little bear becomes a household pet, roughhousing with the children and licking their faces. It's part of the family.

But the bear grows, and its animal instincts grow too. It begins winning those playful bouts, pinning the family members, and hurting them. It swipes a claw at one of the kids and bites the hand of another, drawing blood.

Soon the family has a difficult decision to make. While they love this bear like a family member, they must recognize that it's a wild animal too. It has caused some damage and it's sure to cause more. What should they do? At the very least, they have to leash it, perhaps cage it. It might be wisest to get rid of it entirely.

The Internet is that bear. It's in your home—practically a family member!—but it's causing damage. What should you do about it?

Coming Home
Sarah and John

Sarah and John had hit a crisis point in their marriage of nearly twenty years. After agonizing over the decreasing frequency of sex in their marriage, Sarah discovered that John was viewing Internet pornography late at night before he came to bed. Though he promised to kick this habit, and he tried to make love with her more frequently, she was deeply wounded.

A swirl of emotions affected Sarah whenever they tried to have sex. She was turned off by the thought of sexual relations with a smut addict. What would he be thinking as he touched her? She was insecure about her own ability to be desirable sexually. After all, he had been watching the pros. And yet she feared that if she stopped sleeping with him, John would go back to using the Internet to meet his sexual needs.

John was very caring and kind about Sarah's insecurities about having sex. He never pressured her or made her feel guilty. He seemed truly sorry.

Sarah decided to take on the role of cop. She learned more about the Internet and shut down their old Internet account, switching to a Christian provider that claimed to be able to block access to pornography. This seemed to be working. Their sex life had not really improved, but at least John was going to bed at the same time she was. That was a huge comfort to her.

One day, cleaning out the back closet, Sarah came across an unmarked video tape. *Hmmm*, she thought. *Strange to find a tape here.* With a sinking feeling Sarah took the tape down and hid it in one of her dresser drawers. She planned to watch it later to see what was on it, but several days went by before she could bring herself to view it. She finally gave the tape to a male friend of hers to review. He let her know that it was indeed a pornographic tape, as she had feared.

Sarah held on to the tape for a few more days. She really could not decide what to do about it. She had believed that things were improving in her relationship with John, but this—it broke her heart. Choosing the passive route, she laid the tape on top of the trash can. John ignored the tape, and eventually Sarah found it in the trash. If he wouldn't come clean, she would have to confront him. "You said it was only the Internet!" she complained. John didn't respond except to agree with her that things needed to change.

Sarah's next role was passive observer. If things were going to work out, she told John, he was going to have to make an effort. And he did, continuing with his positive affection and cuddling, going to bed when Sarah did, and spending more time with her. In spite of the episode with the tape, things seemed to be on the mend.

For her part, Sarah joined a group for women whose spouses are sexually addicted. Sarah was shocked when she learned the seriousness of the issues that other women in the group were facing—from child pornography to homosexual lifestyles. She was a little encouraged about her own situation. It could have been worse.

Then Sarah began obsessing that her husband was finding a sexual outlet with a live partner. There was a new woman at John's office, younger than Sarah and very attractive. Sarah found herself constantly comparing herself to this woman. What could she do to look younger or thinner? She had had two children and she was forty years old, but still she berated herself mentally for not living up to expectations. Sarah started having a difficult time getting out of bed. She stopped going to the support group, because she felt that her problem had nothing to do with what they talked about each week.

One night, after Sarah had been asleep for a few hours, she woke to find John's side of the bed empty. Walking into the study, she found John in his old perch at the computer. Reflected in the glass of the window behind John was the graphic picture. "I couldn't sleep," John said casually as he clicked and closed the picture.

Sarah absolutely lost it, screaming and sobbing all at once. All of the pain, anger, and insecurity poured out of her. John tried to console her, but she would not allow it. Her ranting escalated uncontrollably. She felt she could not go on this way. She talked of killing herself because she simply could not endure the fear and shame. Finally John broke in. "Maybe we should see a counselor." Right then, in the middle of the night, John went downstairs and looked in the phone book for a counselor.

When they went to the counselor a few days later, they were enormously helped. One of the big problems the counselor addressed with them was communication. They had never known how to ask each other for what they wanted sexually. It had taken years for Sarah to question John about their sex life. And there were feelings John had been bottling up for years as well. One reason many men turn to porn is the lack of intimacy. When your "partner" is an array of pixels on a screen, you don't have to open up about your problems. It's an easy outlet for men who have trouble with real-life communication.

So Sarah and John worked on the basics of talking and listening. As they began to share their inner lives with each other, a new intimacy grew. They actually began to make love more often.

While things were getting better, they both knew the pornography problem was always just a few clicks away. At Sarah's insistence, they subscribed to a better Internet service, which truly offered limited access, screening out pornography. In addition, they both joined support groups, one for porn addicts and another for spouses of porn addicts.

But it's still a struggle for them. Their home—like anyone's home—is constantly bombarded by sexy commercials, magazine ads, and TV shows. Often John feels the lure toward pornographic images. Sarah sees the same ads and feels insecure about herself. But they're working on it. They're talking about the struggles and they're reinforcing their love for one another. In short, Sarah and John have regained their marriage.

```
six[
```

Are You
Addicted
to the
Internet?

The Test

Check your answers to the following questions:

1. Do you typically lose track of the amount of time you spend on-line?

    ___ yes   ___ no   ✓ maybe a little   ___ not sure

2. Are you sneaking around or hiding what you are doing on-line?

    ___ yes   ✓ no   ___ maybe a little   ___ not sure

3. Do you find yourself obsessed with thoughts about how you can get on-line or when you will have the next opportunity to get on-line?

    ___ yes   ✓ no   ✓ maybe a little   ✓ ___ not sure

4. Do you argue with your spouse or other family members about time on the Internet?

___ yes ___ no _✓_ maybe a little ___ not sure

5. Do you try to keep secret the sites you are visiting?

___ yes _✓_ no ___ maybe a little ___ not sure

6. Do you spend less time with your spouse because of your on-line activities?

_✓_ yes ___ no ___ maybe a little ___ not sure

7. If you have Internet access at work, has your time spent on-line affected your job performance?

___ yes ___ no ___ maybe a little ___ not sure

8. When you go on vacation or are away from Internet access for a week or more, do you find yourself preoccupied with finding a way to get back on-line or get back home to your computer?

___ yes ___ no ___ maybe a little ___ not sure

9. Do you do or say things on-line that you would not want your spouse to know?

___ yes _✓_ no ___ maybe a little ___ not sure

10. Are you confiding in an on-line partner or saying things to him or her that you wouldn't say to your spouse?

___ yes _✓_ no ___ maybe a little ___ not sure

11. Do you find yourself becoming aroused while on-line?

___ yes _✓_ no ___ maybe a little ___ not sure

12. Do you seek sexual stimulation on-line?

___ yes _✓_ no ___ maybe a little ___ not sure

Discussion

Any self-test is limited by your own judgment. It tells you what you tell it. For that reason, we've avoided any kind of numerical scoring. The purpose of this test is to give you a sense of the danger signs. As with many addictions, people can ease into Internet dependency without realizing they're hooked. In drug terms, the Internet is more like Valium than heroin. It has a valid purpose that may disguise its addictive properties. So maybe this is a moment to step back and look at your life or to urge your spouse to do that. What signs of Internet addiction are seen in your home?

If you answered yes to just a few of the questions, the Internet probably isn't much of a problem—yet. You can lose track of time (question 1) while bowling or bathing, so that in itself isn't a big deal. But if it becomes so common that it affects your marriage or your work (questions 6–7), then it's a problem. Virtually every family argues over computer use (question 4), but if you find yourself bullying your kids so that you can visit your chat room every night, you may need some help.

Question 1

Do you typically lose track of the amount of time you spend on-line?

Randy remembers his first encounter with SimCity, a computer-game classic that has spun off many variants. In this game the player builds a city—zoning it, landscaping it, and building roads, power plants, and stadiums. Year by year, the city grows as you tinker with taxes and deal with disasters. Once you get the hang of it, you can play for hours. And Randy did, starting at about 9 P.M. one evening. The next thing he knew, it was 4 A.M. Where did the time go?

Many Internet users routinely have the same experience. Some are involved in simulation games or fantasies of various sorts (MUDs or MOOs) that can stretch on for days, even weeks. Some play computer games with on-line friends. And of course others spend huge amounts of time (as we've been saying throughout this book) in chat rooms or in gathering information of various sorts.

There is nothing intrinsically wrong with spending time on-line. We hope we've made that clear. It's only when time on-line overflows its proper boundaries that you run into problems. For instance, in the nonweb world, a man might go with his buddies to a football game and come back six hours later to his loving wife. She doesn't like football, and frankly she didn't mind getting him out of the house for a while. There's no problem there. We all need to take time doing fun things, and some of these fun things we'll do with friends other than our spouse.

How is that any different from the guy who spends six hours playing John Madden Football over the Internet with a friend across the country? There's no problem, as long as his wife doesn't mind the time away from her and as long as he was *planning* to spend six hours on the game. If he was planning to play for, say, one hour, but got into it and couldn't stop until the wee hours of the morning, that's a problem.

So it's not just a matter of the time you spend; it's your *control* over the time you're spending. If you often find yourself saying, "Where did the time go?" you should start exploring tactics to regain control of your computer time. Alarm clocks, buzzers, and strict rules (no Internet after 1 A.M.) may help you. If you ignore these reminders, you have a deeper problem.

Question 2

Are you sneaking around or hiding what you are doing on-line?

Genesis tells us that Adam and Eve hid from God after they sinned. If God wasn't already omniscient, that would have given him a clue as to what they had been doing. When we do wrong, we try to hide it. And if you feel guilty about your Internet activities, chances are you'll find a time to get on-line when you can hide away from your family—in a den, some corner where no one's looking over your shoulder, late at night, when everyone's asleep. This is common in the stories we've been hearing about Internet addiction.

If you've somehow steeled yourself against the idea that your activity is wrong, at least take a look at your sneaky behavior. Shouldn't that tell you something? "But it's not that I feel guilty," you may protest. "It's just that my spouse wouldn't understand. *That's* why I have to sneak around." You've got a point there. We don't hide our behavior only when we're doing something wrong; we also hide when we fear that someone else might disapprove. But that opens up a whole new can of sauce. Why would your spouse disapprove? Isn't that something you should talk about? If it's a misunderstanding, then clear it up. Isn't it your job to help create an atmosphere of mutual trust and love in your marriage? Then why would you hide something from your spouse, especially if it is perfectly innocent?

One of the best ways to keep a budding addiction from blooming is to be open about it. Turn on the lights. Be honest about what you're doing. If you develop accountability with your spouse and with others in your life, you will be less tempted to step over the line. Secrets allow all sorts of problematic behavior to develop; a policy of openness will help curb unacceptable behavior.

City planners have found that a crucial deterrent to crime is good lighting. When setting up an area of operation, criminal gangs often shoot out the streetlights. It's just like Jesus said:

> They loved the darkness more than the light, for their actions were evil. They hate the light because they want to sin in the darkness. They stay away from the light for fear their sins will be exposed and they will be punished. But those who do what is right come to the light gladly, so everyone can see that they are doing what God wants.

> John 3:19–21

You might say the same thing about your Internet behavior. Quit sneaking around and come to the light!

Question 3

Do you find yourself obsessed with thoughts about how you can get on-line or when you will have the next opportunity to get on-line?

When a drug addict moves to a new area, the first task is to find a local pusher. When you're hooked on something, you have to ensure a steady supply of it. The addiction becomes the center of the addict's life, and everything else revolves around the fix. Oh, there are addicts of all kinds who hold down jobs and carry on social lives, but those things aren't central. The main thing is to feed the addiction.

Addicts feel normal when they are "under the influence." That applies not only to drug and alcohol addiction but also to most behavioral dependencies. If you're a compulsive gambler, you just don't feel right when you're not gambling. You don't have to be gambling all the time, but if you're not gambling, you are preparing yourself for your next big play. It's always on your mind—when and where and how you'll be able to gamble again.

That's how it is with Internet addiction as well. Remember Evelyn who spent fifty hours a week on the family computer, chatting on the Internet? She had a full-time job, but her husband and kids report that she ran to the computer the moment she got home from work. You can bet that many hours of her working day were spent thinking about getting back on-line.

An addiction grows tentacles. As it takes hold of someone's life, it infests with its power and influence every part of the life. It's not just the drug that tempts you, it's the needle, it's the street corner where you get your stuff, it's the sight of someone on TV who looks like your pusher. It's not just the gambling, it's the daily lottery numbers on TV, it's the sports report, it's the quarter in your hand that reminds you of your first slot machine. We form associations in our brain, and they're hard to sever. When your Internet addiction gets bad, you can hardly touch a computer, see a screen, or hear the crackle of a connecting fax machine without obsessing about your next visit to cyberspace.

That's why the most severe cases require cold-turkey abstinence from the Internet and perhaps even from computers in general for a while. You have to escape those tentacles.

Question 4

Do you argue with your spouse or other family members about time on the Internet?

Some families argue about everything, from who sets the table to who handles the TV remote. If your family is like that, it may seem natural to fight over the computer and Internet time as well. You may have other needs for family counseling, but this doesn't necessarily indicate an Internet addiction.

People argue about what's important to them. Chances are you're not fighting over the old eight-track tapes in your closet, because you really don't care about them anymore. But if you are addicted to the Internet, you will insist on using the computer as much as possible. Forget the kids' homework. If your spouse wants to e-mail your in-laws, tough! You need that machine!

Any addiction takes one ordinary thing and balloons its importance. We see this especially with behavioral addiction—compulsive gambling, eating disorders, even shopping too much. There's nothing wrong with eating a piece of chocolate, but when eating chocolate becomes the most important thing in life, it's a problem. Even gambling wouldn't be a big deal if you went and blew ten bucks on the slot machines. Hey, it's a form of entertainment. But it's hard to stop gambling. You blow ten bucks, and you'll waste a hundred more trying to get it back. Gambling becomes the most important thing to you in those moments, more important than food, than financial security, than your family.

Of course, the same pattern occurs with the Internet. In small doses, it's harmless. But it gains immense importance as a person becomes addicted to it. You *must* get on-line, and woe to anyone who would prevent that. If you've barked at your spouse or kids lately because Internet use has become way too important to you, take it as a warning signal.

Question 5

Do you try to keep secret the sites you are visiting?
We discussed some of the implications of hiding as we dealt with question 2, but this comes at it from a

slightly different angle. Are you in the habit of quickly clicking on a different window when you hear someone approaching? There are miniprograms that can change your screen at the touch of a button, hiding any private material you've got there; have you invested in one of these? Do you regularly clean out your cache of temporary Internet files, cookies, and history, so no one else with access to your computer can track your surfing? Have you bought firewall protection to keep on-line snoops from seeing your activity?

If you've made these or other attempts at hiding your Internet activity, you need to ask yourself what you are trying to hide. Granted, some firewall protection may be wise if you're working with sensitive financial, business, or personal issues. But do you really need to be so surreptitious with your family or coworkers? The answer is yes only if you're going places you shouldn't go.

We may step on some toes here, but we think it's sort of like radar detectors in cars. Some states have outlawed them, but even if they're legal, can you think of any clearer admission of guilt? It's like putting a sign on your windshield: "I'm going to exceed the speed limit regularly, so I use this gadget to keep me from getting caught." In the same way, if you have made specific attempts to keep from getting caught in unscrupulous Internet use, that's a pretty clear indication that you're doing stuff you shouldn't do.

Question 6

Do you spend less time with your spouse because of your on-line activities?

What's the most damaging aspect of Internet addiction? You could make a case for the sexual fantasy of on-line pornography use or some steamy chat, which certainly violates the precious sexual bond between husband and wife. You could say it's the misplaced intimacy that many web users find with chat partners, sharing deep things that ought to be shared only within the marriage union. But the most basic problem, even among those who stay chaste in their on-line activity, is the inordinate amount of time that addicts spend on-line.

One of the major obligations of marriage is being there. Tom has counseled numerous couples and many others who have gone through divorce, and one consistent theme emerges. Couples get in trouble when they stop spending time together. Sure, some couples have more individual independence than others. We've known two-career couples that commuted to New York and D.C. and still had successful marriages—but only because they recognized how important it was to make the most of the precious time available for each other. They're still the exception to the rule.

Last year a professional athlete turned down a trade from a losing team to a contender because his family was settled, and he didn't want to have to move away from them. Fans were outraged, but we cheered his decision. Time spent with your family is vital to their health and yours. You must not take it lightly.

But let's qualify this a bit. Sometimes a husband or wife can be there without being there. They sit in the same room, perhaps at the same table, but they're not really participating in family life. The same could be said of the Internet addict who sits in the same house with his or her family but goes into a private room to surf the web. That's not being there. You have to be available. Look at all the "keep out" signs you've put up—the private room, the closed door, the grunts of disapproval when you're disturbed. If you want to conduct innocent business on the Internet, fine. But open the door. Let your family know that you *can* be disturbed. Show them that they're more important to you than your on-line connection.

Question 7

If you have Internet access at work, has your time spent on-line affected your job performance?
This has become a huge problem in many businesses. The Saratoga Study of Workplace Internet Use recently found that 64.3 percent of the companies it surveyed had reprimanded or disciplined an employee for inappropriate use of the Internet. Pornography was the biggest culprit—41.1 percent had problems with employees viewing pornographic sites—but on-line chatting (12.5 percent), games (11.6 percent), sports (8 percent), investing (7.1 percent), and shopping (6.7 percent) were also problems for some companies. Note that these figures involve only the people who got caught. No doubt even more than 64.3 percent of companies are losing employee hours to the Internet without being aware of it.[1]

Employees have always found ways to waste time, but now it's easier. The time-wasting machine is right there on the desk. You have to use the Internet for your work anyway. Why not detour through a few porn sites?

Some of this can be attributed to a bad attitude about your job. Many people seem to operate with the basic rule: Do as little work as you can, without getting fired. Corollary 1 states: Try to make it look like you're working really hard, without actually doing so. The full-time job of the people who follow this philosophy is to stay a step ahead of the boss. When they hear the footsteps in the hallway, they have just enough time to switch to a work-related web site.

Some companies are wising up and investing in ways to monitor their employees' computer use. Amazingly

119

there are some legal challenges to these methods, citing invasion of privacy. Seems to us, if you're on company time, on a company computer, the company has a right to make sure you're doing company business.

But we can't blame the whole crisis on bad attitudes. We know people who really want to do an honest day's work, but they can't withstand the temptation of the Internet. They might start on their lunch break, exploring some interesting sites, but the next thing they know it's 3 or 4 P.M. and they're still surfing, while their project of the day goes undone. They make all sorts of excuses: "I have to know how to navigate the Internet"; "I have to see what the competition is doing"; "This porn site is doing amazing things with graphics." But ultimately they see that their Internet addiction is stealing hours from the job they get paid to do.

Question 8

When you go on vacation or are away from Internet access for a week or more, do you find yourself preoccupied with finding a way to get back on-line or get back home to your computer?

A few years ago Randy took a vacation in a beach town and found a cozy little Internet café just down the road. This was a great help, since he had taken some work with him and needed to e-mail some clients. An added benefit was that he enjoyed the atmosphere—a hot cup of java and a light sandwich sitting next to the mouse pad. When he returned to the same vacation spot the next year, he went down the road to his old Internet haunt, only to find that it had gone out of business. This was a crisis. How could he stay in touch with the wider world?

Searching the Yellow Pages, he found a listing for another Internet café twenty miles down that beach-hugging road. It wasn't a bad drive, but it took almost an hour to get there. Still, it was worth it to stay in touch with friends and clients via e-mail, so he made the drive a couple of times during the week. On the last day of his vacation, Randy happened to take a walk in the other direction, and he found an Internet café about a block from his hotel. If only he had known!

While Randy isn't exactly addicted to the Internet, he would still have to answer yes to question 8. By itself, this question doesn't indicate web addiction, but it does point up a potential danger area.

One key determination of addiction is the severity of withdrawal. Can you do without this? Whether it's drugs or alcohol or gambling or web use, it's common for addicts to say, "I can quit anytime I want." The best answer to that is, "Okay, try it."

If you're not addicted and you quit for a while, you're just taking a vacation from a habit. If you are addicted, you will suffer serious withdrawal symptoms. Our recommendation (for you and for us) is to take advantage of your next vacation to go Internet-free for a while. The worst that will happen is that you lose touch with people for a week or two. But isn't that sort of the idea of a vacation? On the other hand, it may reveal that your Internet addiction is worse than you thought, and it may help break a behavior that had become far too habitual.

Questions 9 and 10

Do you do or say things on-line that you would not want your spouse to know? Are you confiding in an on-line partner or saying things to him or her that you wouldn't say to your spouse?

We're back to the issue of hiding. Maybe you've never had to hide your activity because your spouse takes no interest in the computer. This is often the case with couples middle-aged and older. For younger people, it's just part of the culture, but older folks didn't grow up with computers, so it's possible that one partner has gone on-line while the other remains blissfully ignorant. Still, if you find yourself typing or viewing things you'd want to hide from your spouse, that's a danger sign.

These questions are especially helpful for those who get involved in chat rooms. Most porn viewers know they're doing wrong, but chat rooms can be more seductive. You may start with the purpose of making new friends, and you do that, but soon you find yourself complaining about your spouse. Your chat friends are taking your side against your spouse, perhaps even heightening the problems. "He interrupts you when you talk? How dare he! That shows total disrespect for who you are. You should just go off some weekend without him. Let him wonder. Show him the same disrespect he shows you. That'll teach him." And so a bad habit becomes grounds for divorce. Instead of raising the issue with your spouse, you let the chat room whip you into a frenzy. It doesn't always happen like that, but it can.

And we've already seen some examples in this book of chat room pals who became illicit lovers. We don't have transcripts of their chats, but they probably started with innocent friendship. At some point, they began saying things on-line that they wouldn't want their spouse to know. This drove a wedge between their Internet life and their married life, and they never recovered.

But shouldn't you be allowed to confide in a friend? Everyone has complaints about his or her marriage, even if they're minor ones. Don't we all need to blow off steam sometimes? Isn't it good to express our frustrations to a trusted friend? What does it matter if that friend happens to be on-line? This line of reasoning makes some sense, but we must be very careful about it. First, marriages need good communication. If there are problems, they should be raised within the marriage. Talk about the issues. See a counselor. Get those frustrations ironed out.

Still, we recognize that there are often little quirks that irk you. They may not be worth a major marital confrontation, but you still need to blow off some steam about them. Be extremely careful about the "trusted friend" in whom you confide. We would strongly recommend that this confidant never be of the opposite sex. And we doubt that you would ever find anyone this trustworthy on-line. (Not that on-line people aren't trustworthy, it's just that you don't know how trustworthy they are. Don't take a chance on someone you know only through typed messages.)

Questions 11 and 12

Do you find yourself becoming aroused while on-line? Do you seek sexual stimulation on-line?
These questions are pretty obvious. If you answer yes to them, it's likely that you're addicted. But let's start with a not-so-obvious angle. Some people get a near-sexual arousal from their addictive behaviors. Compulsive gamblers report a euphoria when they place a big bet. Overeaters often compare food to sex. We're suggesting that Internet activity—even if it's just checking stocks or scores—can provide true addicts with a rush that rivals sex, as certain chemicals are released in the brain, providing pleasure. If this is your experience, then you almost certainly have an addictive tendency with regard to Internet use, and you need to be careful about overdoing it.

123

Of course, if you're viewing porn sites, arousal is the whole point, isn't it? Don't try to tell us that you're a connoisseur of the beauty of the human form. There are museums for that. Some men draw the line at swimsuit or lingerie sites. They won't let themselves view hard-core pornography, but isn't arousal still the object? And doesn't this lust and fantasy still poison your marriage?

As we've said before, the arousal from chat rooms can be subtler. Of course some sites are all about sexual fantasy, but others promote conversations that might lead anywhere. Some chatters play around the edges of arousal. They find a certain excitement in on-line flirtation. Face it. If a woman's husband hasn't looked at or listened to her for ten years, she'll find some thrill in an on-line partner who flatters her. That thrill can easily become sexual arousal and fantasy.

Question 12 zeroes in on actual sexual stimulation. Do you engage in sexually explicit chat? Cybersex, they call it: "Oooo, baby, here's what I'm going to do to you." Do you fantasize about sexual activity with your chat partners? Do you masturbate while on-line?

Such activity hurts your marriage. Do we even need to say this? It also violates your marriage commitment. We've heard some people wonder whether it constitutes adultery, strictly speaking, since you're not actually touching anyone but yourself. Well, if it doesn't, it comes awfully close. In Matthew 5:28 Jesus warned about lustful looks. Lust-laden cyberchat isn't much different. We'll let you work out the legalities with God, but we can tell you that cybersex in its various forms wrecks marriages. When you find sexual pleasure at a computer rather than with your spouse, you're looking in the wrong place.

Are you addicted? Is your spouse addicted? Your answers to these questions may be yes, no, maybe a little, or not sure. This whole phenomenon is so new, it's often hard to come up with black-or-white answers. Whether or not you'd call yourself officially "addicted," the remedies suggested in the next few chapters may help your marriage.

seven[

Cold
Turkey

Date: 9/18/00
Time: 8:38:37 AM
Remote User

My wife and I have been married for 23 years, and until 9 months
ago, "all was well." I stumbled innocently into a job-related chat
room, on a large Internet jobs web site. Before long, I discovered the
appeal of chatting—starting with people who tell you what a nice
guy you are, how much they appreciate your wisdom and kind
words. . . . Unfortunately I also got in over my head, went to the far
extremes, taking my laptop everywhere, staying up late at night, logging on every weekend, and getting caught up in a larger-than-life
relationship with a very appealing woman. . . . Anyone who thinks
this can't happen, has rocks for brains. . . . I'm fortunate, in that my

wife is one of that small percentage who wants to stick by me and help me get over this nonsense. I'm going to give it all I've got not to let her down.[1]

There's nothing fancy about our basic prescription for addiction. Tom has counseled many who have suffered addiction in various forms, and we've written about relationship addiction and stress addiction. We've had friends who struggled with alcoholism and drug dependency. Whatever the addiction is, the therapy starts with the same bit of wisdom: Stop.

It's never easy. Addictions grab hold of you, changing your understanding of what's normal. It feels wrong somehow to *not* be feeding your addiction, but that's exactly the commitment you need to make. Stop using. Make a clean break. Just say no.

We understand the complications. Substance abuse creates a physical dependency that might require medical treatment to break. Other addictions have deep emotional roots that must be dealt with. But it ultimately comes down to a personal decision to break free of the addictive behavior. Jesus once asked a blind man, "Do you want to be healed?" That sounds like a strange question—until you've encountered people who *don't* really want to be healed. Many addicts really love their addictions. While they may seek help to alleviate the effects of their lifestyle, they really don't want to be entirely clean. Our world has plenty of drug users who have gone through extensive programs to be healed of their chemical dependency, but then they start using again. Sprung from their prison, they've walked back behind the bars. Why would this happen? Because addictions—even the most gripping of them—aren't just physical, they're willful. At the most basic level, addiction is a matter of the will.

This doesn't mean we lack sympathy for those who struggle with addictions. It's tough! But addicted people still must take responsibility for their choices. They can't wait around for someone else to remove the temptations. They must learn to say no. But isn't addiction a disease? Sometimes. That still doesn't remove a person's responsibility. The question remains: Do you want to be healed? If so, then do whatever it takes to participate in your own healing.

Internet Addiction

Throughout this book we've been talking about Internet addiction. While this addiction doesn't have the physical components of drug addiction or alcoholism, it does seem to be a serious behavioral addiction. This thing we're calling Internet addiction is actually several addictions rolled into one. Overuse of chat rooms can develop into a kind of relationship addiction or love addiction. Of course pornography use is addictive to many, and Internet porn douses that fire with lighter fluid. Even tamer Internet use—sports or stocks or simply surfing—can become addictive, as people spend many more hours on-line than they intended. The rush they get from extended Internet use is similar to that of, say, compulsive gambling or shopping.

In 1996 psychologist Kimberly S. Young presented research on Internet addiction at the annual convention of the American Psychological Association. Her study involved nearly five hundred heavy net users. Almost four hundred of them were classified as "dependent." These people, Young reported, "exhibited significant addictive behavior patterns. We also discovered that the use of the Internet can definitely disrupt one's academic, social, financial and occupational life the same way other well-documented addictions like pathological gambling, eating disorders and alcoholism can." In fact Internet addiction seems closest to pathological gambling "because it involves failed impulse control without involving an intoxicant." Young even developed a ten-question survey to determine Internet addiction, similar to the questions we asked in the last chapter.[2]

Are you addicted? The self-test in the last chapter will help you evaluate your situation. If you decide that you are, then our advice at the beginning of this chapter applies to you: Stop.

Yes, the addiction is a powerful force. Yes, the temptations are great. And, yes, you probably need outside help—certainly from your spouse, possibly from a counselor. But no one else can break the power of your addiction. In an act of your will, you just need to stop.

Internet Adultery

Imagine a man who gets caught cheating on his wife. Embarrassed and penitent, he gets on bended knee before her. "I'm so sorry, dear. I promise I'll be totally committed to you from now on. In fact I promise you that I'll sleep with other women only twice a week, absolutely no more than that, okay?"

You think you know this guy, don't you? Well, it's completely hypothetical, we assure you, but it does make a point. To be "totally committed" to a wife requires "forsaking all others." Cutting back on infidelity isn't total commitment. You have to renounce infidelity entirely.

We can say the same thing when one spouse has a problem with Internet use. It's not only an addiction; in a way, it's also an affair. Maybe you're hooked on chat rooms, divulging your innermost feelings to new friends you've never seen. Maybe you download pornographic images and fantasize about the hot bodies you see there. Maybe you just spend so much time on the net that you hardly ever see your spouse. In any case, you're stealing your heart, your desires, or your time from your spouse. The one you're married to has dibs on all of that, but you're offering it to others.

On-line advice columns are generally hit-or-miss, but we found a good one that offered some wisdom on this matter of excessive Internet use. A woman wrote in saying her husband was caught up in chat rooms. "My family seems to think it's harmless . . . but I feel very left out. As soon as he comes home from work he is on the Internet and he doesn't come to bed until three in the morning."

In her response, Dr. Gayle Peterson cuts to the chase. "Your husband is having an affair with the Internet. No wonder you are upset!" A hobby is one thing, but a hobby that keeps you from sleeping with your wife is quite another. Peterson suggests that the couple talk together (asking, "What is he sharing with others that you want or need more of?"), spend more time together, and seek counseling.[3]

Moral nitpickers love the Internet because social ethical standards haven't yet caught up to the new technology. "It isn't really adultery," they say, "because it's only cybersex. We're just talking, not touching." Well . . . okay. But, as we said before, don't you have an obligation to steer your marriage clear of any such obstacles? Sure, wedding vows can get weird these days, but they usually don't include "to honor and cherish, and to make sure I only *talk* sex with others and don't actually *touch* them." You can carve the legalities any way you want, but if you're typing a detailed description of how you'd like to caress someone other than your spouse, it's safe to say your marriage is in trouble. You are cheating.

Whether you call it adultery or cyberadultery is another matter, but you are clearly dishonoring your spouse.

Internet Idolatry

A consuming passion for the Internet can be an addiction and it can be adultery. It can also be something else—idolatry. Normally we don't go looking for spiritual explanations for emotional issues. We've known too many people who slap a Bible verse on a problem and expect it to go away. We believe that God has created us with complex thoughts and emotions and that the most severe emotional problems require psychological expertise.

But addiction is a strange beast, because it is, by its very essence, religious. The addict "worships" the object of his or her addiction. Life revolves around it. The drug, substance, or behavior seems to give meaning to the addict's existence. It is the lord and master of that person's life—in most cases a cruel and destructive master, but a master nonetheless. Some have even indicated that the root of addiction is a "hunger for God."

Brent Curtis and John Eldredge write:

> Whatever the object of our addiction is, it attaches itself to our intense desire for eternal and intimate communion with God and each other in the midst of Paradise. . . . Once we allow our heart to drink water from these less-than-eternal wells with the goal of finding the life we were made for, it overpowers our will, and becomes, as Jonathan Edwards said, "like a viper, hissing and spitting at God" and us if we try to restrain it.[4]

So we can say that Internet addiction, besides being a form of adultery for a married person, is also a way of worshiping a false god. Please note that we're not saying that *using* the Internet is idolatrous, just that the *addictive* use of the Internet resembles idol worship in key ways. If you are addicted to Internet use, you are bowing at a false altar, you are devoting time and energy in the service of this force that promises you fulfillment, and you are placing less importance on the other aspects of your life.

The "spiritual significance of addiction," says Gerald G. May in *Addiction and Grace*, "is that we try to fulfill our longing for God through objects of attachment. . . . We seek satisfaction of our spiritual longing in a host of ways that may have very little to do with God. And, sooner or later, we are disappointed."[5]

This is one reason for the many examples of religious conversion curing addictions. People need the help of a "higher power" to kick an addiction, because that's the whole point of being addicted in the first place: You're seeking a higher power. And when your addiction proves to be a harsh lord, you need a better one.

A Real Addiction

We are trying to make a strong case about Internet addiction because the initial response that addicts routinely have is *denial*. Not me! I'm not addicted. Your answers to the self-test in the last chapter could be off the charts, and you'd still be denying your addiction. If you'd ever reach the point of admitting that yes, you do spend quite a lot of time on the Internet, you'd also protest that it's not that big a deal, it's just a hobby, and your spouse spends time on other things, so what's the problem?

The problem is that it's probably addiction, adultery, and idolatry rolled into one. It's serious business. You need to take drastic steps to break free of it.

You may find it interesting to note that the stages of responding to one's own (or a spouse's) addiction are similar to the stages of grieving for a lost loved one. You begin with denial, then progress through anger, bargaining, and depression, until you finally accept that you have a problem and decide to change it. The stages don't always progress neatly, in order, but they can usually be identified. After denying your addiction for a while, you may begin to admit it, but with anger toward yourself, God, everyone who helped cause your addiction, and the addiction itself. Bargaining involves efforts to cut back on the addictive behavior, trying to manage it in a healthy way. This never really works, and when it doesn't, depression sets in.

Wherever you are in the process, we're not trying to scold you. But the sooner you move out of denial, the sooner you can deal with the problem. You can beat Internet addiction, just as people have defeated all sorts of other addictive behaviors, but it's never easy. It requires willpower, wisdom, and outside help.

And that brings us back to our basic prescription: Stop. If you're addicted to the Internet, just stop using it. Cold turkey. In case you think we're unrealistic legalists, take note of the lead sentence in a news release from the American Psychological Association: "If being online is threatening your job or ruining your marriage, you may have to remove your computer, modem and internet user manuals from your home—similar to the drastic steps an alcoholic takes when he/she throws out all the booze."[6]

The Cold Reality of Cold Turkey

It will certainly be difficult to remove your computer or disable your modem, especially if your work involves

Internet use or if you depend on it to maintain important friendships. For that reason, we suggest several basic questions to ask as you consider this step.

Is It Possible?

Given your present employment, your family situation, and your children's computer needs, is it really possible to remove your computer, as the APA suggested? You may even have a job that requires you to be on-line most of the day. As we said in the early chapters of this book, the Internet is rapidly becoming a fact of life in our society. Increasingly many necessary aspects of life are shuttled through those wires.

But instead of listing all the reasons that it's not possible to go cold turkey, think about how it might be possible. If it were absolutely necessary for you to avoid Internet lines entirely, if they emitted a death ray that would instantly kill you, how would you have to change your life? Your company certainly wouldn't get rid of all computers, but perhaps you could be shifted to a non-Internet position. Or you could find another job. Your kids might still have to get on-line to complete homework assignments, but could they do this at the library? Or could you keep a personal computer in an open area of your home, where you can't be alone with it? Correspondence and shopping could certainly be carried on the old-fashioned way.

Granted, these are major changes we're talking about, but they would be possible if it were a life-or-death situation. And maybe this is. Internet addiction may mean the death of your marriage, unless you take strong steps to protect yourself. It's not uncommon for people to move or change jobs to accommodate their spouse. Here we're talking about saving your marriage. Are you ready to do what it takes? Some people have sworn off computers, at least for a time, because of carpal tunnel syndrome. Is Internet addiction any less serious? The immediate pain may not be as great, but the potential consequences can be far more devastating. Is it so unreasonable, then, to suggest major life changes as a way of combating your addiction?

If it's truly necessary to take certain steps, it's amazing what turns out to be possible. And that leads us to the next question.

Is It Necessary?

We hesitate to ask if it's necessary, because the true addict will probably say no. It's a bit like asking, "Are you in denial?" If the answer is no, it just confirms that the true answer is yes. But the truth is not everyone who uses the Internet a lot is addicted to it. Even Dr. Young's study of "active Internet users" found that 100 of the 496 people studied were *not* "dependent," that is, addicted. We also feel that there's a spectrum of Internet dependency, more so than with drug addiction or alcoholism. Some are mildly addicted, we might say, while others are deeply dependent. A mildly addicted person may be able to keep his or her computer job, for instance, as long as certain boundaries are observed, with proper accountability.

So this question could be rephrased. *How much* change is necessary? To determine that, you have to go back and consider not just whether you are addicted, but how much. Start with the questions in the last chapter. If you gave positive answers to only two or three of the questions, you probably have some "issues," but you're not addicted and major life changes aren't necessary. On the other side of the spectrum, if virtually every question seemed to be targeting you specifically, if you answered yes or maybe to nine or ten of the dozen questions, then you need to get serious about this situation. You're a web junkie, and major changes will be necessary to break your dependency on the Internet. If you're somewhere in between, you may be considered "somewhat dependent." In this gray area, you'll still have to take some strong steps, but the strongest—actually getting rid of your computer—may not be necessary. Stopping Internet use cold turkey will still be helpful for the mild or moderate addict, but certain exceptions can be made.

Besides the admittedly simple self-test we offered, how can you tell how addicted you are? Ask people. Go to the people around you that you trust most. Give them the details of your Internet use and ask for their opinion: How addicted are you? Definitely talk with your spouse about this, but it may help to have another friend weigh in as well. To get an impartial opinion, you probably want to ask someone other than your on-line chat pals.

With serious addictions, friends and family often stage what is called an "intervention." This is designed to shock the addict out of denial. Basically a group of people who care about the person are brought together to confront that person about the problem. One person can be shrugged off, but a surprise party of your favorite people gathered in your living room to warn you to shape up—that's a jolt. In most cases like this, the person would admit to having a *mild* problem with the object of the addiction, but nothing that can't be handled. The intervention shows the addict just how serious the problem is.

If you think you may have an addiction to the Internet, but you're not sure how serious it is, you can sort of do your own intervention by asking for the opinions of trusted friends and relatives. If your spouse is the one who's addicted, you may want to try something like an intervention, but be careful. First, be sure to talk about the problem with your spouse, then perhaps with only the immediate family present. Suggest marriage counseling too. If your spouse refuses to go to a counselor with you, see a counselor yourself to review your options. If your counselor thinks it would help, he or she may help you set up an intervention.

The whole point is to come to an understanding of how serious the problem is and what steps are necessary to defeat it. Addiction doesn't occur in a vacuum. It affects your marriage and your whole family, if you have kids. The remedy will require teamwork from everyone involved. So it makes sense to talk together about the extent of the addiction and what steps should be taken.

Is It Advisable?

Considering the complexity of the issue and your own point on the spectrum of addiction, what sort of remedy makes the most sense? Is it advisable to give up the Internet altogether, or will that cause more problems than it solves? Could you give up the Internet temporarily? Are there certain boundaries that could be drawn between legitimate Internet use and illegitimate use? How can you set up such boundary lines so they won't be crossed?

We want to be completely clear. We believe thoroughly in the "just say no" concept. The best thing anyone can do for any level of Internet addiction is to stop all use of the Internet, at least for a while. If a person is strongly addicted, this is absolutely necessary, even if it's impractical. At mild or moderate levels of addiction, however, exceptions can be made. Cold-turkey cessation is always helpful, but it's not always necessary, and if you're in certain jobs or locations, it may not be advisable. In these cases, you'll need to develop a system of Internet management that will keep your use of it under control.

Severe addiction: Cold turkey necessary, even if impractical.

Moderate addiction: Cold turkey helpful, recommended. If extremely impractical, other measures can be taken.

Mild addiction: Cold turkey helpful, but if it's impractical, try other methods.

One way to determine both the necessity and the practicality of cold-turkey cessation is something we call "Try it; you'll hate it."

For a certain period of time, perhaps a week or a month, experiment with your lifestyle. Try avoiding the Internet entirely. If your job requires that you use the net, you could try this method while on a vacation, or just avoid all nonbusiness use of the net for that period of time. Decide in advance how long this experiment will last, and stick to it. Imagine you're going on a cruise for that period or on a wilderness hiking trip. Your on-line pals will be there when you return. A few weeks shouldn't be a great hardship for you.

Then, from time to time during this period, take note of how you're doing. Is it hard to stay away from the Internet? Do you think about it constantly? What are you doing instead of going on-line? How is this experiment affecting your family life?

This experiment can show you a lot of things, but the most important thing is the seriousness of your addiction. Here's a simple formula: The harder it is to stay off-line, the more you need to. You may not realize the intensity of your addiction until you experience the withdrawal symptoms.

If you can't make it through your trial period, you are probably suffering a severe addiction. If, during the last few days of the experiment, you find yourself thinking nonstop about the joy of getting back on-line, you have at least a moderate addiction. If you have little problem with the trial period, sometimes even forgetting about the Internet entirely, then you have no more than a mild addiction and perhaps none at all.

The experiment can also show you some things about the practicality of lightening your Internet involvement. Some people say, "I couldn't live without that connection!" Well, you probably can. People lived just fine before the Internet. There are lots of things in our lives we see as necessities that are, in fact, unnecessary. If you had to, you could probably function without a car, a TV, air conditioning, or indoor plumbing. And if, because of a serious addiction that's damaging your marriage, you have to function without the Internet, you probably can. The short-term, cold-turkey experiment can teach you that. If nothing else, the experiment begins to break a habit that has begun to dominate your life.

In the next chapter, we'll discuss alternatives to cold turkey. Are there ways of living with the Internet without letting it rule your life?

eight⌷

Living
with the
Web

Subj: Lunch tomorrow
Date: 5/15/02 9:48:36 PM Eastern Daylight Time
From: Drew66@hotmail.com
To: smpp100@aol.com

Lunch tomorrow is fine with me, if the offer still stands.

Sorry I haven't responded earlier. I just read my e-mail for the week.
If you've made other plans, I understand.

For what it's worth, I'm trying to cut back on the Internet for a
while, so I'm just checking my e-mail once a week, every Wednes-

day night. It was just becoming way too important in my life. I can tell you more about it at lunch.

Oh, and if you need to change any of the arrangements, just give me a call. Remember that phone thing, collecting dust in the corner? :)

It's as simple as a-b-c-d. Well, of course it's not simple at all, but if you have to have the Internet in your life and you still struggle with addictive tendencies, there are four conveniently alphabetical principles to remember: accountability, boundaries, change, and displacement.

Accountability

There's a paradox about addiction. On the one hand, it's a lonely life. Addicts engage in a private struggle, trying to hide their actions from friends and loved ones, attempting to summon strength to withstand temptation but failing time and time again. No one quite understands what the addict is going through, except for other addicts.

That's the other side of this paradox. Addicts of all sorts gather in societies of the similarly addicted. Alcoholics have drinking buddies. Drug users often shoot up or snort or smoke with others. Gamblers love the casino crowd. There is a sort of communion, with a gallows humor about their shared servility: "How bad was your hangover?" "I got so stoned that I . . ." "Guess how much I lost at the tables."

Paradoxically their addiction is both public and private. We see the same contradiction with Internet addiction. As we've already noted, Internet use is pretty much a private activity. The computer is usually in a nook big enough for one user, with one chair, one mouse, one keyboard. It's just physically difficult, in most setups, to gather the family around the computer. That may change as computer technology merges with TV technology, but at this time computer use is a solo sport. And so any addiction involving the computer is a private matter.

But it can also be social, which explains the appeal of chat rooms. People want to connect with others who understand them. If you're a heavy user of the Internet, where are you going to find other users? On the Internet, duh. So sometimes you have people chatting via Internet about how they're spending way too much time on the Internet. It's the society of the similarly addicted.

The irony is that net addicts often *detach* from the people who know them best—spouse and kids—in order to *attach* to their cybersociety. They feel misunderstood at home and so they reach through the wires to others who share what's most important to them—the Internet. It's a resocializing, just like the teenager who starts hanging out with the wrong crowd. Old friends are scuttled and new friends adopted.

In fact the classic image of the wayward teen makes a pretty good comparison for some of the Internet addicts we've met. Gail, who chatted with teenagers, seemed to be going through an adolescent-like self-discovery. In the process, she rejected her real-life family in favor of web friends. You can almost imagine her as a pouting teenager complaining, "You don't understand me anymore. The kids I hang out with let me be who I really am."

And it's true in a way. The teenage "gang" won't scold her for drug use or missing curfew. They let her do whatever she wants—not because they love her more, but because they love her less. Her family cares about her, so they hold her accountable for her behavior.

The same situation can be seen in the chat rooms. People pretty much let you be whoever you want to be, because they have no real stake in your life. You might make the adolescent decision to withdraw from your family to hang with this new crowd, but if you expect the chat room crowd to love you more, you'll be disappointed in the long run.

True love involves accountability. And if you're serious about taming your Internet habit, you need to set up accountability relationships with those who love you most. Accountability simply means that you agree to account for your actions with another person. This rips the veil of privacy off your addictive activities. If you spend too much time on the Internet or visit sites you shouldn't or develop relationships on-line that compromise your marriage, your accountability partner has a right to know about it.

Obviously, choosing the right accountability partner is crucial. It's great if this can be your spouse, but if your marriage is already in trouble, this might be dangerous, because the normal process of holding someone accountable could be misunderstood as nagging or prying or judging. So if you're on shaky ground, don't risk it. We suggest an "open door policy" for all marriages with regard to web use, but in troubled relationships heavy-duty accountability isn't always advisable between husband and wife.

What about relatives? Maybe, but be careful here too. Basically any relationship that has a lot of baggage is a bad place to set up accountability. Most people have some sort of emotional issues with their parents. Siblings can be very good as accountability partners or very bad. You want people with whom you can be completely honest, people who won't judge you by their own standards, only by the standards you set up with them.

Look for a friend like that. If you're a Christian, do you need to find another Christian as an accountability partner? Not necessarily. Sad to say, many Christians are judgmental, making it tough for you to be honest about your failures. Sometimes a non-Christian can be more encouraging. In general, since you're dealing with marital issues along with your Internet issues, look for a friend of your own gender. There are exceptions, of course, but it's dangerous to bare your secrets to anyone who could be seen as a rival to your spouse.

Once you've selected your accountability partner, you need to ask the person to fill that role. It's not a casual task. As you explain it, you may want to say something like:

Here's how I'd like to live . . .
Here's how I'm living now . . .
I'd like you to check up on me [every week? every day? twice a week? every two weeks?] to see how I'm doing and perhaps to pray with me for God's strength.
My commitment to you is complete honesty—even when it's embarrassing.
I ask you to encourage me but also to remind me of the kind of life I want to live. You can scold me when I screw up, but I ask that you respect my privacy and not tell others what I divulge to you.
I believe I can trust you in this. Will you help me?

Key components of an accountability relationship are honesty, permission, and encouragement. You must be brutally honest even when it hurts, and your partner must be honest in responding to you. It's better to say nothing than to lie.

You must give explicit permission to your partner to ask personal questions and to shame you when you've done something shameful. Most people these days won't

145

do that unless you beg them. They feel they have no right to ask about personal issues and to scold you. You have to give them the right.

Your accountability partner should try to encourage you as much as possible, but this doesn't mean accepting everything you do. If you've screwed up, you deserve a talking-to. The ultimate goal is that you will screw up less and less as time goes by. Both of you must keep that goal in front of you. In a good accountability situation, the mere knowledge that you'll have to answer for your actions is often enough to keep you on the straight and narrow.

The following are questions an accountability partner might ask you:

1. How much time have you spent on-line?
2. Have you done or said anything on-line that you wouldn't want your spouse to know?
3. Has on-line activity kept you from doing anything you should have done with your family or on your job?
4. When have you felt the most tempted to go on-line (when you shouldn't)? How do you fight these temptations?
5. How late at night have you been on-line?
6. What web sites have you visited?

As we've said, spouses are often bad accountability partners. Ideally husbands and wives should be accountable to each other, but this specific accountability relationship requires a high level of mutual trust. If your relationship has been contentious, it may take time to rebuild that trust.

However, honesty will be essential as you rebuild your marriage. That's why we suggest that you counter the privacy problem with an open-door policy. Ask your spouse (and maybe your kids) to visit you as you work on-line, to sit with you and see what you're doing. Set up a love seat at the computer, rather than a desk chair. If you make computer use more of a group activity—and encourage your family to join you whenever they want—you'll create a strong deterrent to on-line misbehavior.

Boundaries

It is possible to use the Internet well, even if you've misused it in the past, but you need to set up and observe wise boundaries. Essentially that's what the problem is in most addictions—a lack of boundaries. One glass of wine won't hurt you, but a night of nonstop drinking will. The overeater is merely indulging in too much of a good thing. You could say much the same thing for most other behavioral addictions—not a problem within certain boundaries, but only when the behavior goes out of control.

So, if you have displayed signs of Internet addiction, see if you can create good boundaries. Begin by looking at the following areas:

Time. Would it be reasonable to spend fewer than five hours a week on-line? You and your spouse can set any amount of time you like, but make sure you both agree.

Curfew. How about never after midnight? Adjust that to fit your own schedule, but note that the wee hours of the morning are the most tempting. As you get tired, your defenses go down, and you're less likely to be interrupted by spouse or kids. It could also be said that the on-line community becomes much more interested in sex chat after hours. You don't need these temptations. Observe a curfew.

Web sites. If you have had a problem with chat rooms, stay away from them. If porn sites have troubled you, steer clear. There are Internet service providers that automatically screen out sexual sites. Your computer also keeps a record of sites recently visited. Learn how to use this, and teach your spouse how to check up on you. (Internet Explorer, for example, has a "history" button on the toolbar.)

Chat subjects. If you love chat rooms but have been drawn into inappropriate conversations, set clear boundaries about the sort of thing you won't discuss. If a chat partner keeps bringing up sexual matters, get out of there. Don't be polite, just log off.

Privacy. As we've already said, your Internet use should not be secretive. So you may need to explicitly *remove* boundaries from the rest of your family. In many homes, it's as if there's an invisible no trespassing sign by the computer. Take that down! You may also want to consider setting your curfew at the time when the last other person in the house goes to bed. Or make it a rule that anyone in the house who goes on-line has to tell someone else.

Priorities. Decide that the Internet will take second place to spouse, kids, friends, job, and so on. When they need you, log off. To remind you of these priorities, you could create "Get off the Internet free" cards and give them to your family, so they can hand one to you when they need your undivided attention.

One of the problems of the Internet is that, considering its newness and the inroads it's making into everyday life, we don't yet have a clear sense of the right and wrong of it. We don't know when to say when. But if you will be whole, if your marriage will be whole, if your family life will be whole, you'll have to find an appropriate place for the Internet. That means you'll have to set up wise boundaries and observe them.

In the wizened wisdom of New England, Robert Frost wrote, "Good fences make good neighbors." You could apply that to your neighborly relations with the Internet as well. You can get along with it fine—as long as you know its proper limits.

To return to another metaphor we've used before, the Internet is a wild animal, ferocious and dangerous. As you set up strong boundaries, you cage this creature. Those boundaries will protect you from destruction.

Change

In this chapter, we're talking about principles that can help you combat an Internet addiction, while still having the Internet in your life.

Our next principle is change. Obviously the cold-turkey renunciation of the Internet would be a major change, as would the boundaries you set up. But there are also many other helpful changes you can make. Some of these changes may seem trivial, but they're still important. You don't need to change only the bad things you do; you need to change the little things that lead to the bad things.

All addictions have triggers. In counseling, as we try to identify these triggers, we think in terms of people, places, and things. (Yes, we realize that you could think of the whole world in terms of people, places, and things, but the point is that triggers can come from anywhere.) Here are some examples:

- A grown woman visits her strict parents and comes home with a strong desire to overeat.
- A man attends homecoming weekend at his old college. He drives by the old hangouts where he used to drop acid and experiences an urge to do drugs again.
- Someone cleans out a drawer and finds an old chip from a casino. This provokes memories of a time of compulsive gambling and an urge to try it again.

It doesn't take much—a momentary image on TV, a song on the radio, a child's comment, a relic in a drawer. These people, places, and things can jack up the temptation to fall back into an unhealthy addiction.

People

The people triggers take three basic forms:

Partners in crime are those people with whom we used to carry on the addictive behavior—drinking buddies, sex partners, poker pals. We may feel a desire to be part of that society again.

Emotional lightning rods are those people who make us feel the feelings that propel us into addiction: anger, desire, pain, confusion, and so on. For many, these emotional catalysts are parents, siblings, or an ex-spouse. You may get through the face-to-face encounters with these people, and then you try to salve your wounds with the old addictive behavior.

Object lessons are people who merely represent something we want, need, or feel. We may not even know them. The classic example here is the male sex addict who sees an attractive woman on the street.

He doesn't know her. There's no emotional baggage. She's just an object of his lust.

Places

The place triggers have various forms as well:

Habitual haunts are the casino, the brothel, the dorm room, the bar, the corner where we used to score our dope. Seeing these places, smelling the scents, and hearing the sounds can fill us with a longing for the "good old days," even if those days weren't really that good.

Similar sites with familiar sounds and smells can reach us elsewhere too. You walk past a building that looks like the porn shop you used to visit. You enter a store in the mall, and the incense reminds you of the pot you used to smoke. Again, it doesn't take much to throw you back in time and into the old temptations.

Stress factories are those places that push us to the point of "needing" our old addictions. We don't actually need those substances or behaviors, of course, but we have associated them with escape, peace, or relaxation, so we're especially tempted in times of stress. City streets, subways, busy offices, crowded malls—any environment that stresses us can push us backward into an addiction.

Things

The things that trigger addiction come in all shapes and sizes—and none at all. We've already mentioned smells and sounds. These can be extremely powerful triggers, but other triggers can be defined in the following ways:

> *Keepsakes* are those items that have been part of our life in the past and, for whatever reason, we've kept them. Now they can remind us of our past addiction.
>
> *Talismans* are objects that carry a certain power, representing something beyond themselves. The poker chip is a good example. On the casino floor, it has value. It's not just a reminder; it's a portal to a new world. We knew a young man years ago with a temporary addiction to arcade games. Whenever he held a quarter in his hand, he felt an urge to play Pac-Man. For an Internet addict, a computer mouse might have that same effect.
>
> *Objects of desire* are merely those things that recreate the old craving. A sex addict may have trouble walking through the lingerie section of a department store. A compulsive gambler may see an expensive car and long for the easy money that would buy it.

The reason we talk in such general terms about addiction is that Internet addiction is a broad combination. Habitual users of Internet porn clearly have a form of sex addiction, while chat room denizens seem to have a variation on love addiction or relationship addiction. Others who just spend too much time on-line often exhibit a thrill seeking that's close to a gambling addiction. Since the problems are so broad, it's hard for us to pin down the specific people, places, or things that trigger every Internet addiction. If you're struggling with such an addiction, you'll have to do some creative thinking as you look for your triggers.

Obviously, people triggers for Internet addiction would involve chat room comrades or e-mail correspondents, but they may also include all sorts of emotional lightning rods or objects of lust or fantasy. The main place trigger would be your computer, at home or in the office, but it may be that any computer could trigger the compulsion. Of course, the Internet is a kind of "place" all its own, and so, as you navigate the web, you may need to watch out for certain sites that remind you of your trouble spots. And thing triggers will include computers and computer paraphernalia but could also be the chair you sit in, the knickknack on the desk, or something you thought about buying on eBay.

As you seek to live with the Internet, we challenge you to change your lifestyle to some extent, avoiding the people, places, and things that would trigger a relapse into a more severe Internet addiction.

If you've been hooked on chat rooms, withdraw from your relationships with the people you met there—don't answer their e-mail. Also be careful about the emotional triggers of your life. If you've just spent a tense weekend with your parents or siblings, understand how vulnerable you are—not a good time to log on.

Consider changing around the room where your computer is. You're trying to make some adjustments, to live by new rules—it makes sense to move the furniture. And be careful about the stress factories of your life. Don't use the Internet as an escape from your stress. As you do get back on-line, stay far away from the sites that would drag you into addiction. If you've struggled with hard-core porn, don't even think about visiting a soft-core bikini site.

You can also use the power of things to keep you within your boundaries. Place a cross, a Bible, Bible-verse plaque, or a picture of your spouse and kids by your computer. Get a mouse pad made from a drawing your kids have done—or something that will remind you of them. The point is you need to make your computer and the things around it a celebration of your family life rather than an escape from it.

As you explore the people, places, and things that have attached to your Internet addiction, even minor changes in your life can help you break the destructive cycle and start a new, more positive pattern.

Displacement

Don't think about pink elephants! That's the classic example that proves our next point. You're thinking about pink elephants now, aren't you? It's hard *not* to think about something when you're trying not to, because whenever you begin the effort to avoid the thought, you have to think about it. We find this true in the attempt to stop bad habits or kick addictions as well. Often the person focuses so much on ending the bad behavior that the behavior becomes all the more important. It can become an obsession.

If you have a nasty habit of thinking about pink elephants, the best way to kick it is simply this: Think about something else. And if you have allowed the Internet to commandeer your life, it will help you immensely if you just learn to enjoy other stuff. After you've set up accountability with a trusted friend, after you've decided on boundaries to keep your web use in check, after you've made those changes of people, places, and things, you don't need to obsess about how much you're using the Internet. Just do some new things.

For a marriage that has suffered from one partner's Internet addiction, those "new things" will be shared activities. You need to shove the Internet off the seat of honor in your life, displacing it with pleasant and thrilling real-life events. You need to restore your marriage, to strengthen it to the point that it is of primary importance, and you don't need Internet images or intrigues or information to give your life meaning.

Of course there are hundreds of volumes written about strengthening marriage. Find good ones and follow their advice. Ask a pastor or counselor or friend to recommend helpful resources. But here, in the rest of this chapter, we'll recommend certain activities that you and your spouse can share, and thus displace the dominance of the Internet in your life.

Talk Together

Talking together is so basic that many couples forget how to do it. Set aside time for just talking, sharing thoughts and feelings, catching up on news of the day. Remember that half of talking is listening. When your spouse is talking, don't just catch your breath or think of your next point—listen. Try to understand where your spouse is coming from. You don't need to argue about everything, but you don't need to agree with everything either. What's most important is that you listen and understand.

Husbands and wives need to understand each other's speaking rhythms and level of emotional safety. In general, women find it easier to talk about their emotions than men do. Many men express their emotions slowly. There are exceptions, so examine how well you and your spouse discuss emotions. Often women get frustrated because their husband doesn't express his emotions. In some of these cases, however, the men have tried but have been frustrated when their wife finishes their sentences for them or reacts before the emotion is fully expressed. Sometimes it works the other way, but in any

155

case both spouses need to provide a safe environment for the expression of emotions. Wives need to be patient as their husbands slowly open up, and husbands need to be more courageous in exposing their emotional core.

As long as we're talking about gender generalizations, let us say that men like to win. And if they find themselves in a losing situation, they'll opt out. Once again, there are exceptions, but consider whether this explains the stalemate in your own relationship. Has the man stopped sharing his emotions because he can't do it as well as the woman can? If that's the case, we can only beg husbands to take a chance on opening up, and we beg wives to give them the chance to do that.

But while we're at it, let's throw some more generalizations around. We ran across a report from the National Institute of Mental Health, which uncovered two factors that often correlate with divorce: "wives who start arguments and husbands who don't let their wives give their opinions and suggestions."[1] That's no big surprise, but it reminds us that marital conversation is a team sport. We all tend to take talking for granted, but it's one of the most important activities in a marriage. If you have been involved with Internet porn or chat room lovers, chances are the conversation in your marriage has broken down. You need to take steps to restore it. Sit down with your spouse and learn how to talk again. It may not even be a bad idea to call a counselor for the specific purpose of getting retrained in the art of conversation.

Play Together

What happened when you were dating? Sure, you talked a lot, but you also did things together, things you enjoyed—movies and dinners, concerts and games, pic-

nics in the park and walks on the beach. It was important for you to have fun doing things in each other's
company. It's part of how you grew together.

Marriage expert Willard Harley calls this "recreational
companionship," and he rates it as one of the major
needs of marriage. Couples should find activities they
both enjoy and then do those things together. We know
a husband and wife who share a crossword puzzle every
night after dinner. Other couples enjoy making dinner
together or bowling or skiing or playing cards. There
are zillions of activities you could share; find something
you both love.

Please note: This is more than dragging your spouse
to the football game or tennis match that *you* want to
see. You both need to be excited about the activity. And
try to make it more than spectator sports. Find some
way to play. Break out the old Trivial Pursuit game.
Learn how to play racquetball. Join a community choir.

The Internet is, of course, a vast playground, but it
tends to be solitary, luring you away from your marriage
and other relationships. You can displace the Internet's
thrills by creating some thrills of your own in real life.

Be Together in Pleasant Settings

Sometimes all the talking and playing are just too
much work. You can also restore a marriage by just
being together in places you love. One problem with
Internet obsession is that you forget there's a physical
world out there. You need to rediscover that world.

Try this: List the five places you love most, and ask
your spouse to do the same. These don't have to be exotic
vacation spots, though one or two might be. You could
list the frozen-foods section at the Acme or the corner
of Fifty-first and Lex at rush hour. It could be your

favorite coffee shop, the open road, your backyard, or Paris.

Take a day or so to compile your lists, then talk about them. What do you like about these places? What do they smell like, feel like, taste like? How do you feel when you're there? Then combine your lists and see how many you can visit together in the next year. Get out your calendar and plan when you can do this. Then do it. Just go to those places and hang out. No need to say or do anything special; just be there together.

Start a Project Together

Get something accomplished by doing a project together. You might choose some bit of home remodeling or perhaps a mutual self-improvement project. Don't choose anything you've been nagging your lazy spouse to do. Pick something new to which you can both contribute rather evenly, and make sure you both pick the project together. Write a book together, learn a language, or build a treehouse for the kids.

Be warned: If your marriage is in serious trouble already, this might make it worse. But if your problem has been neglect rather than animosity, working together on a project will help you get to know each other on a whole new level.

The Internet can be a valuable resource, but users can waste a lot of time there too. As couples work together on positive projects they can gain the satisfaction of time well spent.

Learn to Make Love

It would be easy to say to the man who downloads pornography, "Stop looking at those images and have sex with your wife." Or we could say to the woman who's caught up in sexually explicit chat rooms, "Stop fantasizing about your web partners and be sexually intimate with your husband." But it's not that easy. There are always underlying issues that drive people to these fantasies.

However, if you are trying to strengthen your marriage and forget such fantasies, one of the best things you can do is develop a satisfying sex life with your spouse. And so we suggest that, besides talking together and playing together and being together and working together, you need to learn to make love together.

Learn? Don't you already know how to do this? Maybe not. Now there are all sorts of guidebooks and manuals that can instruct you on sex techniques, but the best instructor is right in front of you—your spouse. You don't need to become an expert in sexual technique. You *do* need to become an expert in making love to your spouse. You have to learn what pleases him or her. Take the time to talk about it, study your spouse's responses, and learn how to offer pleasure and express your love.

There is often shyness involved, especially among religious folks. They do the same-old same-old year after year without ever talking about it, because "nice people don't say those words." Sex is an amazing gift God has given to be explored and enjoyed thoroughly within marriage. You have not only the right but the *responsibility* to talk about how you can be a better lover for your spouse.

And it's a sad irony that many people, too shy to ask their husband or wife where to touch them or how to please them, will turn to Internet porn or sex chat. They're viewing all sorts of perversions or even typing detailed descriptions of what they imagine doing with their cyberlover, but they can't discuss anything with the one person with whom it would be perfectly appropriate to talk freely about sex.

If that's your story, start getting your priorities straight. No matter how awkward it may be to talk about sex, you need to communicate with your spouse about this important matter. You need to teach your partner how to please you sexually, and you need to become a student again, learning from your spouse how he or she likes to be satisfied.

Can the Internet Serve Your Marriage?

We've been talking about ways to topple the Internet from the throne of your life. If it has been a taskmaster, destroying your marriage, you need to displace it with healthy marital activities. But perhaps the ultimate displacement is this: employing the Internet in the service of your marriage. Are there ways that you can use the information, resources, and relationships of the web to enhance your marriage instead of degrading it? Even if you've had to go cold turkey for a time, completely avoiding the Internet, you might come back to it eventually *along with your spouse.*

Now we're not talking about viewing computer porn together or entering sex-oriented chat rooms together. While those might seem like good ways of sharing your lives, they never turn out the way you hope, and they generally result in more pain, confusion, and discord.

Still, there's a vast array of positive web sites you could visit together. Why not use the immense resources of the web to help you play, talk, work, or just be together? If you steer clear of the potholes, you can travel nicely down this superhighway side by side.

Net Growth
Ruth and Max

Ruth had been knocked for a loop as a result of her divorce and for a while floundered trying to find her way. Eventually she went back to school for a business degree and started a mail-order business from her home. This business became successful, and life began to improve for her dramatically. Yet the pressures of managing employees, overseeing the company's expansion, and planning a new building project provided limited time for a social life. Six years after her divorce, she was ready for a new relationship but had no time for dating, so she turned to the Internet.

Internet dating is always a risky proposition, but Ruth did pretty well with it. She used a service that prescreened applicants, which made the process a little safer. Because the service required background checks, financial records, and references, it protected Ruth from getting involved with a complete fraud.

After several on-line conversations with potential dates, Ruth met Max. He was different from the others—more intelligent, witty, and able to express himself well, at least in writing. She felt that Max could be the one she was looking for, so they agreed to a face-to-face meeting. The service had suggested starting with a casual lunch, which is what they did. They lived about an hour apart, so a halfway point was picked and the meeting was set.

The date went well. Max was as charming in person as he appeared on the computer screen. Ruth was excited. After a few more dates, they began talking about marriage. It was sudden, Ruth realized, but Max was everything she had hoped for. As she began thinking of dating, she had decided she would consider a serious relationship only with a Christian (and Max was) and a working professional (Max was). She also found in Max a level of understanding she hadn't expected. Like her, he had been through a painful divorce. Like her, he had a busy life, which was why he had used the Internet dating service.

The dates became more frequent, though the hour drive was a pain. And three months after they had first met, Ruth and Max got married. Friends were surprised by how quickly it happened and skeptical because of the whole Internet thing. But Ruth and Max spoke highly of their Internet experience and the service that helped them find each other. They never would have met otherwise. And even in their worst moments, they would always be grateful for this blessing.

I (Tom) met Ruth and Max when they came in for counseling due to problems in their relationship. They had been married just under a year and were still getting to know each other.

It wouldn't be fair to blame the Internet for their marital problems, but the fact that they met and married so quickly meant that they had a lot of adjustments to make. Max had been divorced for only two years and needed someone to help him through a lonely time, while Ruth had been too busy to consider dating. Now, as a married couple, they were facing some challenges.

Ruth and Max were both very Internet savvy. For Ruth it was just a tool for running her business. She took many orders over the Internet and spent far too much time answering e-mail and customer questions as a hands-on manager. After the wedding Max turned out to be much less busy, as his business was in a lull. He was content to stay home much of the day and chat on-line and surf the net. This was a source of conflict for Ruth. She didn't trust him and his use of time. After all, he had met her on-line. Would he meet someone else? And why was he content to live on her earnings? Why wasn't he more ambitious?

"She's too busy for me," Max complained. "Even when she's home, she just logs on and then works all evening." He was already feeling bad about himself. Her busy schedule and success only made him feel worse.

In short, there was a lack of trust and no real understanding between them. Ruth was more driven in her business than Max wanted, and Max was more laid back than Ruth would have liked. Helping them was a matter of going back to the beginning of the relationship and establishing a firmer foundation. As in any marriage, they needed to understand and accept each other, even with their differences.

Ruth's goals in counseling were to find a better balance between her work and her relationship. Before marriage she didn't have to consider anyone else, and her work schedule offended no one. But now she had to learn to shut down the computer and put effort into her relationship with her husband. Max expected her to spend time with him every evening. He also expected the house to be cleaned, which was something Ruth expected him to do. (They eventually hired a cleaning service.)

Meals were also an issue. Again each expected the other to take care of the meals. They settled on a schedule that included going out two nights and sharing the meal preparation the other nights. In fact it became an activity they could enjoy doing together at the end of the day.

Ruth's time on the Internet was not an issue for Max as long as she was able to limit her after-hours work. But Max needed to make some changes in his Internet use. As Ruth expected, he was on the Internet too much and was indulging in some risky behavior. He had begun chatting with old single acquaintances. Most of it was innocent, but for an attention-starved man, it didn't take much for him to play with the fantasy of meeting someone new, someone who would be more available and who would make him feel better about himself. Max was able to be honest with Ruth in counseling about how he was feeling and why he seemed so shut down. Eventually he was able to be honest about what he was doing on-line.

Since Ruth was so Internet savvy, Max asked her to hold him accountable for the sites he visited and the conversations he had. (She knew how to retrieve old files, even deleted files.) But, in fact, Ruth never really had to check up on him because once he came clean, she could tell when he was being honest. "All I have to do is look him in the eye and ask him if he had any conversations he shouldn't have had on that day. He has such a strong conscience that he can't look me in the eye and lie."

By the way, Max's answer to Ruth's question wasn't always, "No, I didn't do anything I shouldn't have." There were days when he admitted to her that perhaps someone contacted him and he entertained a "borderline" conversation. And there were days when Ruth slipped back into her old work habits. Both were making progress, however, and growing together in a trusting and maturing relationship. My sessions with Max and Ruth stopped after a year. They had made great strides in their relationship.

Every marriage has its troubles. The Internet merely presents more trouble to get into, and right at your fingertips. Max and Ruth's story reminds us of the dangers and possibilities of the Internet. It's a tool that has become part of their lives. Ruth needs it for business. Max coordinates his church's e-mail list, collecting and dispersing prayer requests that go out instantly to all members of the church. They also keep in touch with the missionaries they support. So we don't need to demonize the net. We just need to be careful.

nine[

Help My
Spouse!

www.helptalk.net

Q. My husband has a problem and I don't know what to do. He doesn't want to admit it, but I know he's on-line looking at x-rated pictures several times a week. It breaks my heart. I've worked hard to be attractive for him, but now he's turning away. What can I do? I've tried to give him the opportunity to tell me, but he won't. What makes it especially shocking and embarrassing is that we both are leaders in our church. If this went public, it would be awful. I just have no clue how to handle this.

"I'm a wife. The wife of a porn addict. I'm relieved to know what it is, though I always knew something was wrong. Tears. Pain. Disgust. Betrayal. To face the death of a husband would be better than this. A widow has the support of the church. A porn addict leaves shame and divorce."[1]

That's the story of "Emily," from the last chapter of a book on porn addiction, a problem that has just come to light in the last five or ten years. Previously most people assumed that relatively few men were hooked on porn, and these would be obvious perverts. Now we realize that pornography has enslaved thousands of ordinary citizens and many community leaders. The Internet has made the entrapment much, much easier.

When we began our research for this book, we expected to find many stories of husbands caught up in Internet porn. What surprised us were the tales of wives lured into chat rooms, becoming obsessed with the sexually charged conversations that take place there. In all these situations, there are spouses left in the wake. Spouses who wonder how to deal with this unwelcome new partner in their marriage.

We're calling it Internet addiction, and we've identified three general forms: addiction to Internet porn, addiction to Internet chat rooms and the relationships developed there, and a general addiction to the thrills and possibilities of the Internet. Any of these variations can do a number on your marriage.

One bit of advice: Don't get too caught up in definitions. It may not really matter whether you call your spouse an Internet addict. The simple fact is you have a problem in your marriage. If your partner never spends time with you, crawls into bed at 4 A.M. after surfing the web for hours, and talks dirty in a chat room every night—whatever you choose to call it, that's a problem. Face up to the fact that something needs to change.

Getting Help

What should you do if your spouse is addicted? The first answer is get help! See a professional counselor. Even a book like this won't replace the specific wisdom of a professional psychologist. The key here is to find a counselor with whom your spouse will feel comfortable. Perhaps you've been seeing a counselor of one gender, but your spouse would prefer the other. Perhaps you have received great counseling from your pastor, but your spouse is skittish about opening up to someone who already knows you. Keep all this in mind as you select the right person, and do whatever it takes to get yourself and your spouse seated in front of a qualified counselor.

The rest of this chapter contains things your counselor may tell you, steps you can take on your own, and things to do if your spouse won't go to counseling.

So the question remains: How can you help your spouse with an Internet addiction? That depends on your answer to another question: Does your spouse want help? There are really three possible answers to this question: yes, no, and not yet.

If the answer is yes, it won't be difficult to get your spouse to a counselor. Well, you may still encounter some resistance, since the problem could be an embarrassing one, but you can help your spouse most by pressing the issue: "Let's go get help! If you want to restore our marriage, we need to see a counselor." Be flexible on which counselor you see, but insist on seeking some professional help.

Apart from counseling, you can also help an addicted spouse by working on the a-b-c-d principles of chapter 8. Be sure your spouse is accountable to someone—if not you, another trusted friend. Help your spouse set up boundaries for Internet use. Make changes in your family lifestyle to reduce the level of temptation. And displace the need for the Internet with healthy marital activities. All of this will go a long way in helping a spouse who wants to be helped.

What if your spouse does not want help? What if he or she admits an addiction but resists any attempt to change? In such cases there's not a lot you can do. You can't change your spouse. The best you can do is take steps to protect yourself.

Protect yourself emotionally. Yes, this is painful, but don't blame yourself. The spouse of a porn addict will feel undesirable. The spouse of a chat room addict will feel uninteresting. But be very clear on this. Remind yourself fifty times a day that *it's not your fault.* No one ever drives a spouse into infidelity. Your spouse is responsible for his or her own choices.

Protect yourself morally. We know of wives who have prostituted themselves in order to fulfill their husband's fantasies. They end up degraded and no closer to their husband. Keep your own moral compass in this difficult time. Don't get dragged down into your spouse's sin.

Protect yourself financially. If your spouse is spending your mutual money on pornography or on-line gambling or weekends with a chat room lover, you have a right to protest. Beyond the marriage vows and all that, it's *your* money too! Start a separate checking account, if need be. Make sure your spouse's habit doesn't impoverish you.

Protect your family. Gail's son walked in on her as she was engaging in sexual chat with an on-line partner. It traumatized him. You don't want that to happen. If your spouse insists on continuing in addiction, you can insist that the children be protected from seeing pornography or masturbation. You should also take care in how you explain your spouse's behavior to your children.

Though we don't recommend divorce, we understand it in situations where an addicted spouse refuses to change. The porn user or chat room philanderer is essentially carrying on an affair, even if there's no touching. You could make a case that such continued behavior constitutes abandonment.

But even if the addiction never leads to divorce, you and your spouse might settle into an emotional separation. The point is, if your spouse is choosing to cling to an addiction, you have to create a life for yourself. You might continue to live in the same house, but you will find yourself caring less and less. That's very sad, but it might be necessary.

What if the answer to our original question—Does your spouse want help?—is, "not yet"? The majority of people who struggle with these issues find themselves in this very situation. The addicted spouse is in a process, not seeking help yet but not adamantly clinging to the addiction either.

Process of Recovery

As we mentioned before, the process of addiction recovery mirrors that of grief recovery: denial, anger, bargaining, depression, and finally acceptance and restoration. That means, if your spouse is between resisting and renouncing, he or she may be somewhere on the recovery path.

That's good news actually. The path will lead to an understanding of his or her addiction and, hopefully, to the restoration of a better, nonaddicted life. But the addicted person has to keep moving along the path. Your job as the helpful spouse is *not* to force the addict to the end of the process, just to keep him or her moving through it. We'll give you some pointers later in this chapter.

The interesting thing is that a husband's and wife's progress through the stages may be very different. You may be angry about your spouse's addiction, while your spouse is still in denial. Your spouse may be seeking easy solutions (bargaining), while you're already depressed about the whole thing.

We often see this sort of thing with divorce—one partner works through the stages and decides to leave, dumping the issue on the other partner, who has to begin the whole process. With addiction, it may be the addict's spouse who recognizes the problem and, after a time of denial, becomes angry, tries to bargain, gets depressed, and ultimately accepts that this addiction will not easily go away. The addict may still be in denial the whole time. In other cases, the addict tries to deal privately with the addiction, getting past denial, into anger, bargaining, and depression, without telling the spouse. The spouse may have a vague sense that something is wrong, without fully identifying the problem.

By the very fact that you're reading this chapter, we're going to assume that you're the spouse of an Internet addict, that you already recognize the problem, and you want to do something about it. We know that you may be fuming, seeking quick fixes, or moping. All of these are valid emotional steps in the process. Let's first focus on each of *your* stages before we move to your spouse's. Here, briefly, is how you'll feel at each stage:

Denial—There is no problem.

Anger—I don't deserve this problem.

Bargaining—This problem can be easily fixed.

Depression—This problem will never be fixed.

Acceptance—I can deal with this problem.

Restoration—My life will improve in spite of this problem.

Denial

"Houston, we have a problem." There is no shame in recognizing that a problem exists, even if your spouse is trying to hide it. It's natural to want to think that everything is hunky-dory when it's not. Even when people see that a problem exists, they often try to downplay it.

Denial serves a purpose, much like physical numbness when we've been injured. It gives us time to prepare for the pain. Temporarily denial is a great gift, but if it carries on for a year or more, it's unhealthy. It's time to move on.

Anger

It is natural to lash out in anger at your addicted spouse, at the Internet, and at everyone in your path—even yourself and God. Don't scold yourself for being angry. Anger is based on your sense of not deserving what you're going through, and that's probably true. But if you *stay* angry for more than a few months you're getting stuck. Perhaps a counselor can help you move through the process.

Anger serves a purpose in calling attention to a problem and focusing our response. But anger often spills out, hurting innocent people and escalating conflicts. "In your anger, do not sin," the Bible says. Let your anger energize you, but don't go overboard.

Bargaining

Bargaining is the most interesting stage but the hardest to understand. Here's our favorite definition: Bargaining is seeking microwave solutions to crockpot problems. In the bargaining stage, we try to find quick fixes.

In a way, bargaining is a half step back in the direction of denial. It minimizes the extent of the problem. "Oh, we'll just take a second honeymoon!" "I'll just get one of those web site filtering programs." Or even, "We'll just go and see a counselor." All of these may be valuable remedies, but they won't fix the whole problem by themselves. Prepare yourself for a protracted battle against the problem. There will be no quick fixes.

Depression

When you realize that bargaining is futile, you get depressed. When the last ounce of denial has been stomped out, when you face the problem full on, that's depressing. You feel sad, defeated, hopeless.

Depression stinks, but it's also the best place to be so far—because it's closer to acceptance. We don't want to be corny, but it's the darkness before the dawn. Only by staring at the awful face of the problem can you learn how to defeat it.

Acceptance

In acceptance, what exactly are you accepting? This varies according to the nature of the problem. In irrevocable situations, like bereavement, divorce, or terminal illness, you have to accept the sad event and get on with your life as best you can. This is the dawn after the darkness.

In the case of addiction, marital crises, and other issues that can be addressed and improved, acceptance takes on a different light. You are accepting the challenge of facing a formidable foe. You finally realize that it does no good to deny the issue, rage about it, minimize it, or let it defeat you. You have to deal with it.

Acceptance isn't the end of the process. It's the beginning of the battle.

Restoration

Restoration can also take various forms. In the case of divorce, it may involve forgiveness or at least a commitment to peaceful coexistence. In the Alcoholics Anonymous motif, it's an ongoing battle being waged one day at a time, with amends being made and quality of life being restored. The addict will always be an addict but a "recovering" one.

In the case of your spouse's Internet addiction, restoration involves new patterns of living. The Internet is either cut out of your life entirely or at least put in its place. Proper priorities are restored. You may recognize that the temptations will always be there, but you—together—are finding ways to manage.

Helping Your Spouse through the Stages

Now we'll go through the stages again, but this time it's your spouse who's going through the process. How can you help your addicted spouse get through all the stages, ultimately joining you in acceptance and restoration?

It's important to remember two things. First, you can't force your spouse where he or she doesn't want to go. If your spouse is in denial, you could put the problem on a billboard in front of your house and your spouse would still deny the problem—until he or she is ready to move on. Your role is nudging. You want to keep your spouse moving through the process, offering gentle pressure at each step.

The second thing to remember is that you can't cheat any of the stages. If a person gets jolted out of denial too soon, he or she may fall back to it later. It would be nice to jump from denial to acceptance, but it doesn't work that way. All the stages must be crossed.

It's not clockwork. The stages don't always occur in order, and there's some bouncing back and forth. We'd love to tell you to expect three months in denial, then one month of anger, then two in bargaining, but it's different for everyone.

Still there's a general progression in the direction we've described, and your job is to keep the process moving. Don't let your spouse get stuck for too long. Now you may find that a step forward seems like a step backward. A man coaxed out of denial will be angry for a while. That won't be pleasant, but it's healthy. A woman who's convinced to stop seeking easy answers to her addiction will plunge into depression. That doesn't seem like a good direction, but it is.

In your coaxing, nudging role, it will often seem as if you're pulling the rug out from under your spouse, but that's your mission. Keep the process going.

Denial

You have to talk about it. Once you sense that there's a problem, schedule a time for serious conversation. "What's going on, honey? Is there a problem in our marriage? Why are you always on-line?"

The general strategy for your confrontations should be I-you-we. Start with your basic I-language:

I'm sensing something strange going on.
I'm feeling neglected.
I'm curious about what you're doing.

I-language is noninvasive. If your spouse is ready to confront the issue, here's an opportunity to do so. However, if he or she is in denial, your spouse will reject your observations and concerns.

Move on to some well-chosen you-language. Communicate love, rather than anger or disappointment. Stick with observations, rather than assumptions.

> *You're not getting much sleep lately. Is everything okay?*
> *You seem distant these days. I'm concerned about you.*
> *That's the third night this week you've spent on the computer. The rest of the family hasn't gotten to see you much.*

At this point, you've presented some issues that your spouse ought to answer. Denial may continue, and your spouse may offer evasive answers or outright lies. If so, you need to move on to we-language:

> *Things aren't good between us.*
> *What can we do to make things better?*

If your initial observations don't carry much weight, you'll have to start gathering evidence. If you've ever watched *Law and Order* on TV, you know that the first half has cops building the case and the second has lawyers proving it. You're in the first half, just gathering clues for an indictment. So take notes. When does your spouse go to bed? How many hours has he or she spent on the computer? If you can track the web sites visited, do that. Lay the case out before him or her and see what happens.

Your spouse is not only the suspect but also the judge. You want to make the case to your spouse that he or she may have a problem, a serious problem that needs to be addressed. You might even ask your mate to take our test in chapter 6 to find out if he or she is addicted to the Internet.

But you really don't have to get your spouse to admit addiction at this point—just that he or she has a problem and that your marriage has a problem. Best result: Your spouse agrees to see a counselor with you. But even if that doesn't happen right now, you've made your case. You've made it a little harder for your spouse to stay in the denial stage. And that's really all you can do right now.

Throughout this recovery process, you can offer your spouse help and hope. And they are keys to success. You must assure your addicted spouse that if he or she takes the risk of admitting there's a problem, you'll be there to help every step of the way. And the message at each stage must include a note of hope. Yes, it's a serious problem, but we can recover from it.

Anger

You've got a fight on your hands. Once you've managed to coax your addicted spouse to admit there's a problem, a firestorm will be unleashed. You may wish for a return to denial.

If your spouse's anger becomes violent, do what's necessary to protect yourself and your children. Move out. Kick your spouse out for a while. You simply cannot tolerate violence—addiction or no addiction.

More likely, your partner will wage war with words. You will hear many times that the addiction is your fault:

If you were more attractive, I wouldn't have to turn to pornography.

*If you were any good in bed, I wouldn't have these
fantasies.*

*If I found you interesting, I wouldn't be spending so
much time on the Internet.*

These comments will really hurt. Your spouse will
poke at all your insecurities, knowing your weak spots.
No matter how bad it hurts, you must stand your
ground. Do not accept the blame, but do not fight it
either. Ultimately it does not matter whose fault the
addiction is. It only matters how you're going to get
beyond it.

Proverbs 15:1 says, "A gentle answer turns away
wrath." Memorize that; you'll need it. It's better not to
return fire, because there's nothing to win. Hunker down
and weather this firestorm.

Your spouse will be angry at you, at God, at the Internet, at the kids, at the dog, and at himself or herself. It
will be a time of squealing tires and stony silence. Your
partner's self-esteem will fluctuate wildly, from "I'm a
worm" to "I'm a good person and no one really understands me." Let the mood swings happen as long as
they're not too destructive. Wear your emotional armor
and hold your tongue.

Many addicts display passive-aggressive behavior. (In
fact the addiction itself is often a manifestation of passive aggression. That is, they're angry about other things
but they don't show it in conventional ways. Instead,
they throw themselves into this unhealthy behavior.)

Passive aggression isn't obvious. The key attitude is:
"I don't get mad; I get even." Passive-aggressive people
don't rant and rave—they sabotage. And they may not
even know they're doing it. Passive-aggressive behavior
includes tardiness, complaining, laziness, and talking
behind your back. Of course the addict is often angry

with himself or herself and may be using the addiction as a form of self-sabotage, "proving" that he or she is worthless.

If your partner is passive-aggressive, you've probably learned already how to see through the smoke screen. It will greatly help your sanity if you understand that the frustrating behavior of passive aggression is just as much a display of anger as a temper tantrum would be. If you're forthright in your response—"I can tell you're angry with me right now"—you can sometimes get past the passivity. Of course that might just unleash aggression. So choose your poison. It's generally healthier for a person to express anger in active ways, as long as he or she is not physically violent.

There's not a lot you can do to calm the anger of this stage of addiction recovery, but you can coach your partner through it—and by all means protect yourself. You will be wounded during this time. Try to shrug off the pain. Don't indulge in your own passive aggression, storing up the hurts for some future revenge. See if you can rise above it. There are better days ahead. We promise.

Bargaining

This stage can be the most destructive to your marriage. When your addicted spouse hits the bargaining stage, you can find yourself used, deceived, and manipulated. You have to stand your ground on the other side of that bargaining table. You can let your spouse wander through this stage, but don't get drawn into the madness yourself.

The bargainer says, "Let me gain control over my addiction. I don't have to give it up totally; I'll just cut back. If I just do this, this, or this, everything will be all right. And if you, my spouse, can do this or this, we'll be in great shape."

Bargaining minimizes the problem and seeks an easy way out. Your role will be that of a realist. You have to recognize and occasionally remind your spouse how serious the problem really is and that there are no quick remedies.

It will not be acceptable for your spouse to "manage" the addiction by downloading Internet porn only once a week. It will not be acceptable for your spouse to engage in Internet sex chat only on Mondays, Wednesdays, and Fridays. As we've said, these activities are like having an affair. They're just not acceptable in any degree.

In the case of moderately addicted people who merely spend too much time on-line (that is, they're not involved in sexual activity), the issue *is* one of degree. You want them to spend less time on the Internet and more with you—so Mondays, Wednesdays, and Fridays might work out well. But in the bargaining stage, even these people can find ways to cheat the recovery process. That's why you need to establish clear boundaries and stick to them. If your spouse tries to shift the boundary lines, don't allow it.

You're going to be forced into the role of "bad cop," and that will put pressure on your marriage. (That's why it's helpful for your spouse to have a separate accountability partner to alleviate the pressure.) Your spouse may try to change the rules and seek your approval to do so. The logic may go something like this: "If the problem is that I'm hurting my marriage by doing this, and I don't want to stop doing this, maybe I can find a way that it won't hurt my marriage. So if I can get my spouse to agree to it, there's no problem."

The classic example of this approach is men who lure their wives into viewing pornography with them. The women are desperate to save their marriage. The men want to have the best of both worlds. But this doesn't work. It's like inviting an 800-pound gorilla to sleep between the two of you. It might be exciting, but it won't improve your marriage. In those cases, the men are bargaining for all they can get, and the women just want to be helpful. But the best help a spouse can offer is a solid stance—no porn, no sex chat, a lot less time on the Internet. Write down the boundaries you've agreed on and pull out that paper when you're losing an argument. Hold to the standards.

An addict in the bargaining stage is a lot like a child seeing how much he or she can get away with. You have to be as strong as you would be in parenting, even stronger. "If you do that again, I'll . . ." Be careful how you finish that sentence. You don't want to be making idle threats. If you threaten to leave, follow through and leave, at least for a while. But take some time on your own to figure out your best responses to your spouse's possible behaviors. If your mate does a, will you do b, c, or d? What options do you have?

Your errant spouse needs to understand the consequences of his or her behavior. If the addictive action continues, it will take a toll on the intimacy in your marriage. He can't expect to be lusting after naked models in the den and then slip into bed with a welcoming wife. She can't expect to be baring her body and soul to anonymous chat partners all night and have her husband serve her breakfast in bed. The unacceptable behaviors make a difference, a negative difference, in the quality of the marriage. It's not a matter of your being a "bad cop." It's just the way things are.

But you also need to recognize the difference between forgiveness and approval. Many misunderstand this. Someone says, "I'm sorry," and we say, "That's okay," or even, "No problem." But if the person truly did wrong, then it's *not* okay, and there *is* a problem. When your spouse slips up occasionally in the effort to kick the addiction, how should you deal with it?

Is your spouse repentant or rebellious? That may be hard to tell, especially since addicts are often great fakers, especially in the bargaining stage. So your response should have two angles: "What you did was wrong, and it hurts. It will obviously have negative consequences. But if you are truly sorry and you work at doing better in the future, I will be there to help you through it."

Extend mercy, but keep the boundary lines in place. Your spouse is trying to push the envelope, to see how much he or she can get away with, so you need to be clear about what's right and wrong and the consequences for wrong actions. Otherwise, since there are no bad results, you're unwittingly teaching your spouse that it's okay to relapse once a week, and then maybe twice a week.

You must allow your spouse to face the bad consequences. If she's up all night in the chat rooms, don't help her save time in the morning getting off to work. Don't keep his meal warm if he skips dinner to go online. Don't lie for your spouse. And if you're so disgusted by your spouse's sexual activities on-line that you can't sleep in the same bed, so be it. Your spouse will keep bargaining for the best of both worlds. You have to make it clear that's not possible.

Jesus talked about forgiving people "seventy times seven" times, but he also told us to be "wise as serpents and harmless as doves." Yes, you need to keep clearing away your resentment toward your wayward spouse. Don't let bitterness grow within you. We all have sinned; you are a struggler too. But you both must also recognize that your spouse's illicit activity hurts not only you but also the marriage and your spouse. Perhaps you can personally reach a point of reopening your heart 490 times or more, but the marriage requires honest commitment from both partners. At a certain point, after five, ten, or twenty relapses, your spouse is making it clear that he or she is not fully committed to the marriage. Maybe you can forgive, but the marriage cannot. That's just reality. Your spouse can't expect to enjoy all the benefits of a healthy marriage when he or she is routinely violating the marriage covenant and abandoning you.

Depression

It's hard to see someone you love hit bottom. It breaks your heart when your spouse's addiction finally comes crashing in. Withdrawal, moodiness, listlessness, cynicism, and often physical illness occur. This is the depression at the end of the line. Hard to believe, but it's the best place to be so far—precisely because it's at the end of the line.

Imagine two mountain climbers struggling up a slope. One says, "I wish there were a way to move faster."

"There is," says the other, pointing downward.

The addict has two directions from which to choose, up the mountain or down it, through the process or backward. It's easy to go back down the mountain, but that will just make the climb tougher. As we talk about recovery, we often mention the slippery slope. Seldom does anyone go through all the stages in order; there is regular slippage. But eventually progress occurs, and the person reaches the cave of depression. This seems like a pit at the base of the mountain, but it's actually a spot just below the crest. You can't see the top yet—you think you're nowhere—but you're almost home.

In the depression stage, a person realizes how pointless the addiction is. This has been the object of his fantasy, the substance of her hopes and dreams, the altar in the temple of desire. Now it just seems stupid.

It's as if you've saved up all year for a vacation in the islands, but the week before you go, a hurricane demolishes the place. You're disappointed. Or maybe you go, and the five-star hotel in the brochure turns out to be a four-stake hut. You're disillusioned. Addictions promise fulfillment but don't deliver. At some point, the person realizes that, and depression sets in.

Wouldn't it be lovely if your spouse got depressed about the addiction and then excited about *you*? Sorry, it doesn't work like that, at least not right away. It would be great to hear, "Honey, I see that my fantasies were pointless and that I have everything I need in you." But don't hold your breath. Remember that there was a kind of "hole in the soul" that made your spouse susceptible to addiction in the first place. It was a hunger for something *beyond*. And then, as the addiction grew, your spouse was buying the lies. "Your humdrum existence is unsatisfying. Come and look at these impossibly enhanced babes, come and talk with these incredibly sensitive on-line friends. Leave your ordinary life and live out your fantasies!"

Now your spouse is learning that the addiction isn't as fulfilling as advertised, but he or she is still operating under the assumption that ordinary life isn't fulfilling either. In fact a kind of nihilism often sets in: *Nothing really matters. There is no fulfillment to be found.*

This will be hard for you to take. If you felt personally put down as your spouse raced after false promises, you might feel even more insulted now. Your spouse is very needy, and you're longing to help, but you can't.

Chances are your spouse is suffering from desire inflation. The false promises of the Internet have left your spouse wanting impossible levels of excitement. Depression is a time of compression of those desires. The air is slowly squeezed out of the balloon as the addict faces reality again. It will take months, maybe a year.

You might think that, once the addict sees the folly of the addictive behavior, it would stop. Not so. Sometimes depression freezes a person in his or her old habits. The addict is not seeking fulfillment anymore, just distraction. He or she doesn't expect porn or sex chat to bring meaning to life but also doesn't have the energy to stop. Depression often brings a state of inertia, in which a body at rest wants to stay at rest and a body in motion wants to stay in motion. If your addicted spouse is used to surfing sex sites every night after watching the nightly news, that behavior may continue, even if he or she is depressed over the senselessness of it.

And it could get worse. In the bargaining stage, a person actively seeks to move the boundaries. "How much can I do without technically being wrong?" But in depression, the person stops caring. "I'm wrong. I know I'm wrong. Sorry, I can't help it. I'm an addict. Nothing can be done."

But something can be done. While you can't "unde-press" a depressed person, you can create an environment where it's harder to do the addictive activity. You, the spouse, have an advantage now, because your addicted spouse has run out of energy. Now is the time to move the computer into the family room, to spend time on it yourself, to unhook the modem, to cancel the contract with the service provider. Under normal circumstances, your spouse might fight you over these changes, but the depressed addict doesn't have that kind of energy. Make that inertia work for you. If you make the addictive behavior difficult, in this stage you can curtail it.

You could also try to celebrate family life around your spouse. Don't try to drag him or her to all sorts of outside activities. Think of your depressed spouse as a slug, situated mostly on the couch in front of the TV, then oozing over to bed, then oozing off to work, then oozing back to the couch. If that's the case, then bring family activities to the couch. Play family games in that room. Have parties. Don't expect your depressed spouse to join in very much, but keep showing the simple pleasures that he or she can enjoy after finally casting off the addiction. In a way, you're in an advertising war. The Internet has had its opportunity to say, "Real life is boring. Look at the thrills we offer." Now that those thrills have fallen short, you have an opportunity to make your case. "Look how rich and wonderful real life can be."

Even if there are no children involved, you can help a depressed person by simply being there yourself. Sit next to that slug on the couch. Remember Job's friends who sat on the ash heap with their unfortunate buddy for a week. They got into trouble only when they started talking.

You will want to cheer up your depressed spouse. Don't expect this to work. Be as cheery as you want, but you just can't jump-start another person's emotions. Depression is like the common cold. You can't cure it; you have to let it run its course, but you can do a few things to speed the process.

Depression often brings physical symptoms with it—headache, digestive problems, aches and pains, susceptibility to disease. If any of these occur, override your spouse's inertia and get him or her to a doctor. Suggest to the doctor that depression may be an underlying cause. If the doctor agrees, he or she may recommend counseling, which is what you and your spouse have needed all along. Your spouse is right at the edge of admitting a need for help anyway. Perhaps a physical ailment will provide the impetus to do so.

There are a couple of other things to watch out for in the depression period. Many addicts in this time find themselves susceptible to other addictions. Plan A didn't provide the fulfillment it promised, so maybe plan B will. Throw one monkey off your back and find another. And if the new monkey is tamer, then maybe that's an improvement. Cross-addiction is very common—they say that AA meetings are filled with smokers. In any case, you'll want to monitor your spouse's alcohol intake. Try to nip any dangerous new addictions in the bud.

Be careful also about self-destructive tendencies. Depression can make some people suicidal. Others find different ways to hurt themselves. If life has lost all meaning, the depressed person may figure there's no use in going on. We say this not to alarm you—comparatively few actually go through with suicide attempts—just to keep you alert to an area of need. As much as possible let your depressed spouse know that he or she is loved and needed.

In general, as we've said, the spouse needs to offer help and hope through the recovery process. Hope is an especially important gift in this time of depression.

Acceptance and Restoration

Acceptance isn't the end of the story. That's merely the moment when the addicted person begins to see clearly. He or she sees the addiction for what it is, takes responsibility for it, realizes that the way out is difficult, but understands that there is a way out. At this point most people realize they need help, and they'll reach out for it. Some are still resistant to seeing counselors, however. This is not necessarily a relapse. They are just independent souls who like to fix things on their own.

Once again, we urge you to see a trained counselor together to work through the restoration process. It's a serious problem, and you need expert help. As the spouse of the addicted person, you may need to lead the way in selecting a counselor and dragging your mate there. If he or she refuses to go, suggest another counselor. If that's refused, then insist that your partner set up an accountability relationship with a wise friend.

In general, the a-b-c-d principles of chapter 8 will be your agenda for the restoration process: accountability, boundaries, change, and displacement. Set up regular checkpoints between the two of you—perhaps every week or two—to see how you're doing.

This is also a time to examine your own behavior. We don't mean to say that you caused the addiction, but any of the dynamics within the family can contribute to the environment of addiction. Let's be very clear on this. You are not to blame, but you can possibly make things better. Consider your own attitudes and actions in the areas of entertainment, sex, intimate conversation, and time spent together. See how you both can create a stronger marriage.

Often a nonaddicted spouse faces major adjustment during the restoration process. You get so used to dealing with an addicted spouse that you've forgotten how to have a healthy relationship. That's why change and displacement are so important. Build new ways of living. And, yes, there will be deep wounds that are still healing. Give them time. You're allowed to have a couple of temper tantrums and self-pity parties along the way. Everything has been about your addicted spouse for so long; now it's time to consider *your* needs. But don't wallow in the issues of the past. Ask God for the strength to forgive and rebuild. You need to move forward into a new kind of life—together.

ten]

Taming
the Tangled
Web

Subj: XOXO
Date:6/18/02 12:18:27 PM Central Daylight Time
From: rlf@iosys.com
To: robroy99@teknet.net

I just wanted to say I love you. It's been a rough day at work so far,
but I kept thinking about you and that made it better. I'll tell you
about it tonight. I hope your day is better than mine. Can't wait to
see you. XOXOXO.

The Internet is now a part of our culture. We conduct
business, education, and relationships through our computer modems. It will increasingly be the board on
which the game of life is played. There's no getting

around that fact. We all will need to learn how to use it properly.

We're not back-pedaling on our previous recommendations. If you have a problem with Internet addiction, in any of its forms, stay away from it. Find ways to pull out of the Internet frenzy. Don't bargain yourself into a part-time addiction; go the whole way and rid yourself of the problem.

Your abstinence from the Internet will probably be temporary. In a year or two, you may find that you have to get back on-line for legitimate reasons—business, communication, research. And, as we've suggested, you should be okay if you set up and observe wise boundaries—no chat rooms, no porn sites, limited hours on-line, and so on.

But we're wondering if we can turn the Internet from a bad thing to a good thing. Instead of just worrying about staying away from its destructive forces, can we use the web to uphold and enhance our marriages?

That's where this chapter goes. Let's find web sites and Internet-related activities that can draw you and your spouse (and perhaps the whole family) closer together. One disclaimer: We haven't had a chance to peruse everything on every web site we mention. Don't assume that we endorse everything you'll find there. As always, when you surf the net, use your own good judgment.

Giving Intimacy a Chance to Grow

Many couples, especially those who've been married for several years, complain about the loss of intimacy in their relationship. At first, intimacy was very easy to achieve. Everything about the other person was new. At this stage, couples enjoy spending time just sharing their thoughts and feelings. But after the initial honeymoon period, intimacy becomes more difficult. A couple must continue to put time and energy into the relationship or they will lose the closeness they once had. Another problem is that, over the course of a marriage, various hurts and grudges pile up. If these are not effectively dealt with, the result is not only bitterness but also a fear of vulnerability. Couples stop opening up to one another because they're afraid they'll get hurt again.

Restoring intimacy requires time, effort, creativity, and safety. It's hard to achieve all of that with the old "Honey, we need to talk about our relationship." But maybe some enjoyable activities could help you get started. And perhaps the Internet can help you engage in some relaxing and fun times together that will create a nonthreatening environment where intimacy can grow again.

ebay.com

Time: Plan for 2 hours.
Activity: Ask your spouse what his favorite toy was in childhood. Why was it a favorite? Who gave it to him? Then look at this web site, which is a meeting place for collectors of all kinds of toys. Can you find the exact toy your spouse described? How much is it worth now? You can also look up old record albums. Find your favorite songs!

e-mail photos

Time: Plan for 1 hour.
Activity: E-mail your spouse an old photograph of when you were first dating. Tell her what attracted you to her the first time you saw her. If you still live near that place, plan a trip to re-create the scene.

boxerjam.com

Time: Plan for 2 hours.
Activity: This web site has lots of games. From card games to trivia, you can play it here. The site offers you an opportunity to play as a team against other people who are on-line.

expedia.com

Time: Plan for 2 hours.
Activity: Plan a dream vacation together. Pick a destination where you have always wanted to go and assume someone else will be paying. Be detailed. Where will you stay? What restaurants are in the area? What attractions are there to visit? Make up a daily itinerary. When you are finished, total up the expenses. Is it something you want to save for?

e-mail dates

Time: 10 minutes per day, 5 days.
Activity: Send daily hints of where you will go for a Friday night date. Each day give a piece of the driving directions. On Friday send a picture of the restaurant or theater or even a link to the attraction's web site.

christianchatrooms.com

Time: Plan for 1 hour.
Activity: Do you and your spouse have a small, unresolved argument that you need to settle? Go to your peers at this Christian chat room and explain the details, using a he said/she said format. Ask your chat room audience to offer advice, or ask them to vote on how you should handle the problem. Offer to let other couples share their struggles and see if you and your spouse can help them.

e-mail journal

Time: Plan for 20 minutes per day.
Activity: Write a journal entry each day on what you are praying about. Send a copy to your spouse. This is a good way to safely share thoughts and ideas that would be hard to talk about in person.

bnuniversity.com

Time: Plan for 30 minutes per week.
Activity: Barnes and Noble offers free Internet classes. Take an on-line class on how to write a children's book. Write a story together for your children.

highschoolalumni.com

Time: Plan for 30 minutes.
Activity: This web site allows you to register your name and high school so that other classmates can find you. Get out old yearbooks and show each other pictures. What sports did your spouse play? Did your spouse get voted most likely to . . . ?

etrade.com

Time: Plan for 1 hour.
Activity: This web site allows you to trade stocks on-line. It also allows you to create a free account where you can track a portfolio. You don't have to purchase anything to track a portfolio. The site will tell you how much you would have made or lost, if you had made the investment. This is a great way to learn about the stock market. Create a portfolio together. Or you can each create a portfolio and see which one does better. (Of course, if your Internet addiction has involved on-line trading, steer clear of this site.)

Creating Intimacy within the Family

Children can demolish intimacy or re-create it. They certainly change it. Child rearing is a tough job. The biggest danger is spending all of your energy trying to be close to your children and avoiding the sometimes-more-difficult task of being close to your spouse. Time spent together as a whole family can create unity.

Intimacy in your marriage takes time and creativity. The same principles apply when striving for family unity. You need to plan activities that give kids time and opportunity to share their thoughts and feelings.

Discuss ideas with your spouse ahead of time. Use the planning time as an opportunity for developing intimacy as a couple. The easiest thing for the two of you to agree on is probably your love for your kids, so if things have been tense between the two of you, spend time together with the kids. This can be a good starting point before moving to spending time alone.

myfamily.com

Time: Plan for several hours for 3 nights.
Activity: Sit down as a family and come up with a mission statement. What does your family value? Write up the family values and put your statement on your free family web site. The site is password protected so only the people you give the password to can look at or add to it. This is great for spouses who travel or long-distance grandparents. Adding pictures is quick and easy. The site automatically e-mails the whole family when a picture or note is added. Long-distance family members can see pictures instantly.

encarta.com

Time: Plan for 30 minutes once a week.
Activity: Pick a country to learn about, perhaps a place that has current political significance. What do they eat there? How are they similar to our country? How are they different? How could your family pray for the people of that country?

e-mail missions

Time: Plan for 30 minutes.
Activity: Choose a missionary family to support through your church. E-mail them as a family. Print the responses and post them on the refrigerator as a family reminder to pray for them. Learn about the country they live in and explore possibilities of visiting (expedia.com).

myfamily.com

Time: Plan for 1 hour a week until you are done.
Activity: Explore your family history. Put your family tree on-line and make it part of your family web site. Have each child pick a relative to interview about your family history.

expedia.com

Time: Plan for 2 hours.
Activity: Plan a camping trip by picking a state to explore. Locate campsites in the area. Make a grocery list. Look up information on starting a campfire and administering first-aid (askjeeves.com).

howstuffworks.com

Time: Plan for 30 minutes.
Activity: This education site details "how stuff works." This is a great site to explore with children. Learn how televisions work or what makes cars go.

randomhouse.com/seussville/

Time: Plan for 30 minutes.
Activity: This whimsical site is for younger children and it is a good learning experience for first-time web and computer users. Teach children how to use the mouse to click on different Dr. Seuss games and pictures.

flightsim.com

Time: Plan for 2 hours.
Activity: This web site offers free flight simulator software to download. It also offers upgrades to already purchased software. Flight simulators can show you real U.S. cities by giving you virtual tours—a fun and inexpensive way to travel without leaving your living room. Add to the imaginary trip by passing out peanuts and strapping on seat belts.

whitehouse.gov or whitehousekids.gov

Time: Plan for 30 minutes.
Activity: Visit the White House! Talk to your kids about our U.S. president and where he lives. This web site offers virtual tours by the White House dog Spot. Explain to your kids about voting. Ask them whom they would vote for and why.

nasa.gov

Time: Plan for 30 minutes.
Activity: Explore the official NASA web site. Discuss the different programs that are detailed on the site. Choose one mission to follow. Include stargazing trips outside to see if you can get a real-life glimpse of what is detailed on the site.

Saving Time for Intimacy

Several times in this book, we've asked you to "set aside time" to spend with your spouse. No doubt you're thinking, *Obviously they've never seen my schedule!* Maybe you can make time by letting the Internet help you be more efficient in certain matters.

yahoo.com

Time: Plan for 30 minutes.
Activity: This portal web site has a section called My Yahoo. You can program in reminders of birthdays and anniversaries. The web site will send you an e-mail reminder several days in advance. It also provides you with options of free electronic greeting cards, which you can send to friends and family on-line.

quicken.com

Time: Plan for spending 1 hour per week paying bills this way.
Activity: This web site (software must be purchased as well) allows you to pay bills on-line. Quicken works with most major banks. The program will balance your checkbook as well as send electronic instructions to your bank that will write your checks and mail them for you. You can even "memorize" certain bills, such as mortgage payments, and they will be paid automatically. The information is all encrypted, so it is very safe.

screenit.com

Time: Use as needed.

Activity: Preview movies and videos to determine if they have family-inappropriate content.

publiclibraries.com

Time: Plan for 30 minutes per week.

Activity: This site lists all U.S. public libraries that offer on-line services. Most public libraries allow you to search for material on-line and some will collect the books and periodicals for you and hold them at the front desk for pick up. Check the services at your library to see what they offer in the way of time savers.

Repairing Damage to Intimacy

What resources are available that would specifically help your marriage or family life? Various organizations exist with the goal of assisting couples and families, and many of these are Christian ministries. You may want to check into what's available at the following sites.

focusonthefamily.com

The Focus on the Family web site is an excellent resource for a wide variety of solutions to life's difficulties. The section on marriage is broken down by relationship stages, from newlyweds to couples who are trying to maintain the heat. The ideas are very detailed and they are gender-specific. There is a lively and insightful discussion on gender roles as well. The parenting section includes helpful guides like movie reviews. It also displays other parents' views on such topics as trick-or-treating and pop culture. In addition, there is a section called special challenges, which focuses on issues such as homosexuality, ADD, and abortion.

promisekeepers.org

This is the official site of the Promise Keepers (PK) organization, which calls men to be better husbands and fathers. Various resources are available, including a filtered Internet service provider. PK is on the front lines of helping men deal with pornography and sexual addictions.

couplesofpromise.com

Christian counselor-author Kevin Leman *(Sex Begins in the Kitchen)* has started the Couples of Promise organization to strengthen marriages. This site sometimes features live counseling with Leman or Dr. Jay Passavant.

flc.org

This is the web site for the ministry of Dr. Randy Carlson. The site offers free access to parenting articles as well as audio clips of Dr. Carlson's radio program *Parent Talk On-Call*. The site also offers a weekly electronic newsletter.

familydynamics.net

Dr. Willard Harley is the author of several well-known books on marriage, including *His Needs, Her Needs* and *Give and Take*. This web site offers a schedule of weekend seminars as well as a list of eight-week courses. A free on-line discussion of marital issues is also available.

arelationshipplaceformarriageandfamilycounseling.com

This web site offers a variety of quizzes and articles concerning marital issues. Communication and physical relationships are a focus for several of the links. The web site offers concrete steps you can take to improve your marriage.

rejoiceministries.org

Bob and Charlyne Steinkamps run a restored-marriages program through Rejoice Ministries. Their web site includes a bookstore and links to other resources for couples who are separated or divorced.

Readers can access audio clips of the Steinkamps as well as personal stories of people who have been reunited by their ministry. The site offers information on how to join Rejoice Bible studies in your area.

marriageconflict.com

This comprehensive site offers books on every facet of marriage, from conflicts to marriage-building and intimacy. The site has links to larger ministries as well, such as Campus Crusade, Christianity Today, and American Family Association.

marriage.org

Marriage Ministries International (MMI) was started by Mike and Marilyn Phillips, who have been helping struggling couples for more than twenty years. MMI offers a schedule of national and international seminars. This nonprofit organization runs fourteen-week courses called "Married for Life," held in homes. A workbook is available and homework assignments are provided. The site also offers information on how to become an MMI leader.

covenanteyes.com

This site is an accountability program that tracks users' time spent on-line viewing pornography or gambling. Their goal is to inform an addict's accountability partner regarding Internet activity.

Family-Safe Internet

You might find it helpful to subscribe to an Internet service provider that has certain controls, limiting access to some sites. For the most part, these would screen out pornography and sexual content. Here is a list of such providers from Zondervan Church Source.

CleanSurf
CleanWeb

ClearSail
Covenant Promotions
CyberPatrol
EiS Global
FaithHighway.com
FamilyConnect.com
FilterReview.com
GetNetWise
Hedgebuilders
iFriendly
Internet Filter Software
1USA.com
pkFamily.com
SurfWatch

The Internet Family
Alan and Maria

Alan's family is thoroughly modern. They have all of the newest gadgets that a family would want—cable TV, Palm Pilots, cell phones, and several computers with Internet access. But all of these gadgets were creating problems for the family. With two teenagers and one pre-teen, their lives were hectic and heading for trouble fast.

Alan was a busy lawyer, working long hours and some weekends. His wife, Maria, did not work outside the home, but she was very involved in the local school board with meetings several times a week. Their children were all good students, but like most kids these days, they were very busy as well.

The problem in the family was the constant fighting that took place. They fought about almost everything, but sources of constant conflict were the phone, the computer, and the Internet.

It all started about five years ago when both the kids and the technology were younger. Pressure from other kids dictated that their family *had* to get a computer. Alan was using one for the work he did at home, but after much arguing with everyone in the family, including Maria, he agreed to let them use his computer when he wasn't using it. While Alan thought this would appease their demands, it only whetted their appetites. As soon as the computer was available to them, the fighting began. Everyone wanted a turn, and Dad of course needed it frequently for his work. The children complained that the computer was too slow, it had no CD-ROM, did not have a modem for the Internet, and was not available enough.

After constant squabbling, Dad relented and bought a computer for the family. This one was faster and more available, but now all three children seemed to want to use it all the time. The fighting was among the kids now, but Alan and Maria were getting very tired of the arguing. Now the computer allowed them to be on the Internet, but they were using a free Internet service provider. Again the kids found something to complain about. "We need instant messaging, so that we can communicate with our friends!" But this service was only available on AOL and would cost about twenty-five dollars per month.

Alan stood his ground. "You've got everything you need. If you want to talk to your friends, why don't you just pick up the phone?"

But over the next several months, the pressure continued. Compromises were argued and agreed to, but in the end there was always dissatisfaction. What the family really needed always seemed just out of reach. As the technology advanced, so did the needs. Over the next several years, the whining focused on one issue and then another. High-speed Internet access, wireless hook ups, cell phones, and Palm Pilots with all of the accessories—these issues were all negotiated, and Alan often gave in, but he never quieted the troops.

Money was not the issue for Alan, though it was all getting rather expensive. His main concern was the way these devices were tearing his family apart. Everyone *had* to have a personal computer and private Internet access. "Why do you need this all for yourself?" Alan would ask. "Why can't we share?"

The children would offer the classic comeback: "Our friends have even more than we do!" And before long each child's room was outfitted with a computer.

Alan and Maria were fighting a losing battle with their three children. The kids were becoming more disrespectful and more demanding. As they fought over the problems with the children, Alan and Maria were growing more distant as well. Alan began to spend more time at work, just to escape the chaos. He felt frustrated with the problems at home but assumed that it would all pass. His kids were just at a difficult age.

Maria was also withdrawing. She looked to Alan for leadership in these issues, but of course he was not around enough to handle the problems. Maria just put more time and energy into her school board duties.

How did things get so out of control?

The turning point came when Alan's computer was on the blink and he decided to use his daughter's. When he turned it on, it went right to the Internet uplink, which he clicked on by accident. There he found copies of correspondence between his teenage daughter and her boyfriend. He was shocked at what he saw there.

This prompted him to check out his other children's on-line activities. His son, it turned out, was just beginning to explore some sexually explicit material, and both girls were chatting and visiting web sites he and his wife would not approve.

Alan took this information to his wife, who was devastated. While she had been focusing on the school board and what was wrong with the schools today, her own family was demonstrating serious problems. They both confronted their three children in a family meeting.

The parents decided to present a united front, treating this as a family issue that they would confront as a team. Without accusing or embarrassing anyone specifically, they just stated the obvious. Their family life was out of control. Alan and Maria accepted responsibility for letting things get so bad. And for the first time they outlined specific boundaries for the use of some of their gadgets.

They downsized to just one family computer and they put it in the family room. Each child was given a one-hour time slot to use it, but it had to be in front of other members of the family. Cell phones were eliminated, except for Mom's. Her phone was then used when any of the kids went out or had a babysitting job. When the phone was used by the kids, a parent would scroll through and check who was called and for how long. And the kids would need to ask to use the phone at home. Palm Pilots were maintained for schedules and organization only. The wireless connections were disconnected.

It was an adjustment. The kids weren't thrilled about the new rules, but they learned to live without all their electronic devices. All three got involved in after-school sports. Alan got by with fewer gadgets too, and he was glad to see the money he was saving.

Today there's no more fighting about the Internet and the gadgets. They fight about other things sometimes, but in general the home is much calmer. Maria spends less time on her volunteer activities and is more actively involved with the kids. Both Alan and Maria regularly check their kids' on-line activities.

One more thing. Vacations and weekends away are a priority. And one huge rule for getaways—no Internet. This goes for Mom and Dad too. Other than a cell phone for the road, no gadgets are permitted on those tech-free vacations.

Some may think that children need all the electronic tools to keep up with the other students, to live modern lives, to stimulate their creativity, and so on, but Alan and Maria and their family have discovered that they don't need as much as they thought they did.

Notes

Chapter 1 *The Lure of the Net*

1. chatcheaters.com/stories.htm (20 December 2000).
2. Ibid.
3. Steve Watters, *Boundless* (22 July 1999), boundless.org.
4. Steve Watters, "Can Intimacy Be Found Online?" (1999), at pureintimacy.org. Focus on the Family.
5. chatcheaters.com/stories.htm (20 December 2000).
6. Kimberly Young, "What Makes 'Normal' People Sexually Act Out Online?" (10 January 2001), at commitment.com. (Information on Young's research can currently be found at www.netaddiction.com.)
7. Mark Laaser, "Cyber Sex Addiction," *Christian Counseling Today* 9, no. 2 (2001), 39.

Chapter 2 *Not All Bad*

1. "Whole Lot of Clicking Going On," *Christianity Today* (19 February 2001), 17.
2. Ibid.
3. thirdage.com (8 January 2001).
4. commitment.com (10 January 2001).
5. Ibid.
6. Steve Watters, "Online Relationships: Strange Love," *Boundless* (22 July 1999), boundless.org.

Chapter 6 *Are You Addicted to the Internet?*

1. The Saratoga Institute, 3600 Pruneridge Ave., Ste. 380, Santa Clara, CA 95051.

Chapter 7 *Cold Turkey*

1. This is an edited form of an actual message sent to internetaddiction.com/story_log.htm, which deals with Internet addiction.

2. On-line news release of the American Psychological Association at apa.org/releases/internet.html.

3. Gayle Peterson, "An 'Affair' with the Internet?" at parentsplace.com.

4. Brent Curtis and John Eldredge, *The Sacred Romance* (Nashville: Thomas Nelson, 1997), excerpted at pureintimacy.org.

5. Gerald G. May, *Addiction and Grace* (New York: Harper and Row, 1988), 92–93.

6. "Internet Can Be as Addicting as Alcohol, Drugs and Gambling, Says New Research," at apa.org/releases/internet.html, (1996).

Chapter 8 *Living with the Web*

1. *Marriage and Partnership* (spring 2001).

Chapter 9 *Help My Spouse!*

1. Henry J. Rogers, *The Silent War* (Los Angeles: New Leaf Press, 2000), reprinted at pureintimacy.org.

Glossary

cache files: Internet browser programs (such as Internet Explorer) save on your computer some content from every web site you visit. Known as Temporary Internet Files, these help you load those web pages faster the next time you visit.

cookies: Mini-programs an Internet site will store on your computer. Often these just speed the process the next time you visit that site, but sometimes these programs track your other Internet use.

download: To access a document or picture from the Internet and save it on your computer.

firewall: Security measures that keep outsiders from accessing your computer files through your Internet connection.

instant messages: A feature of on-line services that allows a user to communicate immediately to another user who's on-line at the same time.

Internet Service Provider (ISP): A company such as America Online, Yahoo, or Hotmail (and there are many others) that gives you access to the Internet.

modem: The device on your computer that attaches to phone (or cable) lines, allowing you to connect to the Internet.

newsgroups: A type of bulletin board system that allows people to post messages or exchange documents or photos on particular topics.

portal web site: A site that attracts users and then links them to other sites.

spam: Junk e-mail.

virtual reality (VR): The cutting edge of computerization, VR programs attempt to create interactive experiences that seem real to the user.

webcam: A camera attached to a computer that sends live images over the Internet.

webzine: A magazine available over the Internet.

Thomas Whiteman, Ph.D., is founder and president of Life Counseling Services, through which he directs therapists, psychologists, and psychiatrists in fifteen locations throughout Pennsylvania, New Jersey, and Maryland. He is also a director for Fresh Start Seminars, which conducts more than fifty divorce recovery seminars a year. Dr. Whiteman and his wife have three children and live in Berwyn, Pennsylvania.

Randy Petersen is a freelance writer and author or coauthor of more than thirty books, including several on psychological themes. He lives and works in New Jersey.